The Business of Metaphysics and Healing

Dr. Michael Likey, D.D., Ph.D., PsyThD., H.Dip.

DEDICATION

I dedicate this book to my parents Louis and Rachel, whom I know are watching and are proud.

CONTENTS

ACKNOWLEDGMENTS

I would be remiss if I didn't acknowledge all of the healers in all disciplines past, present, and future, whom I have had the honor of meeting. Thank you.

Introduction

Thank-you for buying my latest endeavor. It's hard for me to believe that this makes for my forty-sixth book on Amazon, because it seems just like yesterday that I wrote my first one, *Magic Happens!*

I'm going to be completely honest with you at this point: unless you're a "Gregg Braden", "Louise Hay", "Esther Hicks", "James Van Praagh", "Barbara De Angelis", "Dr. Christiane Northrup", "Sonia Choquette", or any of the other thousands of other famous self-help/Metaphysical healers and authors, you are not going to become famous, nor wealthy. Your motivation, therefore, better be philanthropic, and/or to help your fellow human being, or even better, to help them to help themselves. There is absolutely no room within the Metaphysical field for selfish, self-serving people who are simply after a quick buck.

If you're tired of your regular nine-to-five job or career, and think that you can make your millions by telling fortunes, doing hands-on healing, or even writing a book (especially if you've shown no previous gifts for creative endeavors) about this genre, you can forget this notion as well..

This is because healers, practitioners, metaphysicians, unlike doctors, lawyers, and plumbers, are BORN, not MADE. Sure, you can study Metaphysics and the healing arts, and even mechanically learn how to do "Intuitive" readings, healings, etc., but you'll feel empty inside, even guilty, and eventually abandon your "get rich quick" scheme. Even if you start to do "cold readings", (fake psychic readings) you might fool the more gullible and vulnerable of people, making a dollar or three along the way, but (unless you're a sociopath) you'll either get in trouble with the law and/or have your conscience take over, causing you to give up the ghost, so-to-speak!

Like most artists (take it from me, I AM!) you have some difficulty promoting yourself, for whatever reasons. It's just naturally difficult to promote yourself, especially if you're self-employed and/or fancy yourself an entrepreneur. Everyone needs ideas, inspiration, and motivation to self-promote; in other words, it's hard to be your own agent. Everyone needs some sort of template for success: just like a roadmap to success, everyone needs some sort of tried-and-true layout or plan to move forward in your chosen career, be it music, the arts, and yes, Metaphysics! Doctors, lawyers, and plumbers have tangible services to offer, just like clothing stores and restaurants offer very PRACTICAL and NEEDED products and services! Everyone needs clothing, and a good meal; everyone (at some point or another) needs their toilet fixed, or their house painted! These are NECESSARY and TANGIBLE services; not everyone needs a psychic reading, or a Reiki, or Prana session. Not everyone will turn to meditation or hypnosis in times of need, but instead will (and should) seek out sound MEDICAL advice. But you bet your bottom dollar that when someone wants to stop smoking (for example) or lose weight, they'll turn to a hypnotherapist. When love goes sideways, you bet that many will take the advice of a psychic, as opposed to a therapist, who can help you to find out the root-cause of your problems with relationships...it requires far too much effort!

This is why we often have to MARKET ourselves, in order to convince, or better yet, SHOW and EDUCATE potential clients, how Reiki, readings, or hypnotherapy will be worth their time and money. Hopefully they will feel that they got MORE than their money's worth!

Back in the '70's, '80's and '90's, when I was selling myself (or MARKETING) my graphic designer skills to ad agencies, printers, etc. I showed them how they actually NEEDED me, and that they could MAKE MORE MONEY by hiring me. I used this strategy when selling myself as a magician for restaurants, clubs, organizations, etc., and they actually DID make money from my services by hiring me: people lined up outside of restaurants to see the magician, (myself) who would perform mini miracles at their table either before or after their meal! Once in awhile, I even offered (in print ads I took out) SPECIALS (two-for-one, for example, or 10% off the price of a show "For A Limited Time" with the ad) and this worked well in the "down" season, it was better for me to make $100. (as opposed to my usual $150 fee) rather than nothing, during the quiet times.

What does this have to do with Metaphysics, or selling your metaphysical services to potential clients? When I had a kiosk at a local market offering readings from 1994 to 2000, I had a "coffee card" which I'd stamp every time a client presented this card, (actually my business-card which I stamped on the back) and after five paid/stamed readings, they'd get their sixth for free. Some might consider this tacky. Maybe, but I was the busiest reader in the nearby Tri-Cities area, bringing in for myself hundreds of dollars a day in short, quick tarot readings! As an added promotion/advertisement, I included with each reading ("free") an audio-recording of their reading (on a cassette tape) which I gave them in a clear Lucite case containing my business card! I had no problem eating and paying my rent during those years at the market.

All of this self-promotion or "marketing" might not be your cup of tea, but I had no agent but myself in those days on the west coast. Keep in mind that this is an industry which only recently (in the last ten years or so) has finally gained legitimacy, and "footing", almost right beside the traditional medical healing sciences! Finally, hospitals welcome (gratis) the services of a Reiki practitioner, for example. Traditional Chinese Medicine (Cupping, Acupuncture) is something that many go to for pain relief. Yoga, Tai Chi, and Qi Gong is being practiced by the masses, and is just about mainstream nowadays, as is meditation. All of these are classified under "self-help" and "metaphysics". They are considered "medical arts", "complimentary medicine" and "alternative wellness". Not as frequently anymore is anxiety being treated with drugs, but more with meditation and self-hypnosis; certainly the aforementioned smokers who wish to quit, and those wishing to improve their self-esteem and thereby eat less, consult Hypnotherapists.

There is certainly an abundance of room for qualified therapists, Reiki and Prana Practitioners, and Hypnotherapists. Go out there and get certified/get your degree(s) FIRST in any (and more) of these disciplines, THEN read this book and start working!

I welcome you now, into my world of SELF-PROMOTION, MARKETING, and ADVERTISING as it pertains to Metaphysics and the Self-Help industry.

The reason that I have included suggestions for a Sunday service/gathering, (further on) is because my professional degrees depended upon the registration of my non-profit, society and the holding of regular such meetings. All of my Bachelor, Masters, and Doctorates were earned through the University of Metaphysics and the University of Sedona. If you earn your professional degrees through them (which I highly recommend) then you'll have to do the same and file regular, monthly reports to them, plus pay an annual fee in order to keep your degrees active.

Here are the relevant web links:

https://internationalmetaphysicalministry.com
https://universityofsedona.com
https://universityofmetaphysics.com

Earning professional degrees, entitling you to add initials after your name, is crucial for establishing yourself as a learned scholar and professional in your fields of endeavor; in fact, I would recommend that you get your degrees first, and then write your book(s), in that order!

The first "letters" I earned was my "Master Reiki" certification, and that was all well and fine, but not the same as having earned, say, my Practitioner's degree/Prana certification through the University of Metaphysics. After my Reiki certification, I earned my Clinical Hypnotherapy degree ("H. Dip.") through the Robert Shields College of Hypnotherapy in England. This degree, like the university ones, were Distant Learning Degrees, which essentially means that you download the study material and write exams and thesis/dissertations once you've sequentially passed everything. They are all perfectly legitimate degrees, since the universities physically exist, and have physical addresses which anybody can visit.

In the field of metaphysics, many charlatans and self-deluded individuals exist and practice their art, with no-one to actually regulate their legitimacy, competency, and ethical practices. Therefore, and especially within the field of metaphysics, I highly recommend you pursue the Higher Learning Degrees through the aforementioned universities. I cannot guarantee the legitimacy of any metaphysics degrees you might earn elsewhere, and needless to say, those online "diploma factories" are a no-no! Go on, go for it, you won't be sorry, and you'll increase your knowledge base and also gain many more tools with which to add to your repertoire in order to help enrich other people's lives. If you go all the way and earn your Doctoral Degree, people can also call you "Doctor", or specialist in your field.

Again, here are the links:

https://internationalmetaphysicalministry.com
https://universityofsedona.com
https://universityofmetaphysics.com

If you also wish to earn your Clinical Hypnotherapy degree, here is the link for that: **http://www.hypnotherapy-training.com** Just look at the extensive curriculum:

http://www.hypnotherapy-training.com/syllabus.htm

Societies and Organizations

Once you successfully complete/graduate and earn your degrees, often you may opt to join professional organizations (paying annually their fee) which also look good on your resume, business card, and web-site.

I myself belong to the Association of Professional and Ethical Hypnotherapists, (which you automatically get enrolled into upon successful completion of your degree with the Robert Shields College) as well as the American Metaphysical Doctors Association, which, one is only eligible to join once they've successfully earned their Doctorate through either the University of Sedona or the University of Metaphysics..

Remember: earn your credentials, write your book(s), start a practice, offer workshops and lectures.

Study, learn more, study, learn some more.

3-Seminars, Workshops, & Book-Writing

Let's assume that you've earned your credentials/letters pertaining to the metaphysical industry, and that you've been practicing for several years. "Practicing" means that you are earning a living from, and/or charging professional fees for your services. We'll discuss "professional fees" and specifics later on, but for now we'll take it for granted that you're no longer offering freebies in order to gain the much-needed experience required within this career.

Perhaps you're working at it part-time, but are still getting a professional fee for your services, whether part-time or full-time. Maybe you have an office, (either out of your residence or commercial space) maybe you don't. Regardless, a client comes to you (potentially) to stop smoking, or to lose weight; perhaps they come to you inquiring about helping them with self-esteem issues, or an ache or pain they might be enduring. Perhaps they want to take any one of the courses/workshops that you are offering pertaining to the metaphysical field; you are still demanding and receiving a reasonable, but professional fee, in other words, at par with what other professionals in your area are receiving. At this point (several years in the field) you feel you have a lot to say and to share either with other professionals, or with lay-people. (regular people who might, upon reading your proposed book, become interested in the genre, learn more from the book, and/or wish to seek out your services.) You are ready to write your first book. Wrong reasons to write a book would be, say, if you've just entered your field and wish to garner some more clients; another wrong reason is that you want to get known as an author first, therapist second; I would then recommend that you commit to writing full-time on some other subject than metaphysics until you have new or different information relating to the field, which means getting many years of practice FIRST under your belt! THEN you MIGHT have something to say or contribute to the field! Another wrong reason to write your book is so that you have a "gimmick", in other words so that the public sees you as a therapist who writes self-help books. Again, this isn't not noble, but much experience in the field is required first. Writing a so-called "channeled" book, with no practical source-material to back up your channeled information: this will either prove fatal to you in the eyes of your professional peers, (Hypnotherapists, for example) or actually work in your favor if you wish to go the route of being in some "New Age" genre, which will essentially accept anything and everything if it's well-written. This brings us to the next point: are you a "good writer"? Do you have any professional experience as a writer? Have you ever been published before? Just deciding that you've been "wanting to write" for a long time, and then going for it would necessarily guarantee you success, professionally or other wise! Take some courses on writing, structure, etc. first, so that your book will hold up on a basic level of being "well-written". It's the same sort of drivel I used to hear out here on the west coast when I first moved here: "when I retire, I'm going to start painting!" What, houses? You just don't DECIDE one day that you can paint, draw, or write, you either have a gift/talent for it, or you don't! Then, once you discover that you do, you must HONE your skill(s) to professional levels, before it will be accepted by publishers to be published, or worse, if you self-publish and put it out there without professional honing, your reputation as a professional ANYTHING will be tarnished before you've even left the starting-gate, once people read it.

I went to college to get my professional Graphic Design/Commercial Art certification, for example, which honed my natural drawing gifts to a level where I could at least APPLY to advertising agencies, etc. before they would even consider me to be hired by them. A musician with a natural gift (for violin, guitar, bass, drums, song-writing, singing) must FIRST go to a legitimate MUSIC SCHOOL, and THEN upon successful completion they MIGHT be considered worthy or being employed within the music industry. There are MANY exceptions to this, and MANY who became "stars" without the professional/formal training, but their level of song-writing, etc. is sub-par, but then, who cares? If you love some famous performer's music, voice, etc., that's all that counts! A magician must learn TONS of sleight-of-hand BEFORE they can fool anyone, let alone ENTERTAIN them, and then, do they have a natural talent/comedic gift for timing that will help them to entertain their audience? Only time and practice before live audiences, will hone one's TECHNICAL SKILL, (so that muscle-memory kicks in and one can do sleights for particular tricks/routines without thinking) but as for being a NATURAL ENTERTAINER? That's a whole other thing; there ARE schools of the arts that claim that they can also help to hone one's NATURAL performance/ENTERTAINING skills, so you never know!

I've shared all of this with you so that you might consider your MOTIVATION for writing books, and if you even have any talents/skills to accomplish it all.

Certainly, the commercial value (if the book is well-written) will be of great value along side your metaphysical career, and might even raise the level of professionalism in the eyes of others, including your peers and/or potential clients/students. Writing and publishing a book or books will help you to attain respect amongst others (peers and clients) again, only if it is well-written and informative. This idea of being a self-help/Metaphysical Therapist who also writes books is the ingredient/recipe for success of Hay House and their practitioners/writers. Who are we to argue?

I can only offer you information and advice on how to do this, however doing it well, and at a professional level, is up to you.

Book-Writing

There is a general format/methodology to writing your book, and it's one that I follow as well..

First, you want to write headers, or chapter titles, preferably at least ten. This will be the topics that you'll be covering in your book, and make up the "guts" of your book. They should build to a natural summary and conclusion if you've logically made your case/points properly. Start with the "Introduction", usually numbered "1". Your introduction should include your purpose for writing the book, and what points that will be covered and proven/substantiated, and how. Unlike a thesis or dissertation, you need not list your source material, ("Review of Literature") but of course be familiar with it, with your points and quotes from the material bookmarked for easy reference. Your "case" should build to a logical conclusion. If you wish, you could write the "Acknowledgement" (or "Thanks to") preceding this chapter. I would, and I recommend that you do this. The subsequent chapters will cover the subject-matter of your book. If you want, the last chapters can be titled "Summary", (self-explanatory) and then "Conclusion". (which includes a general thank-you to the readers for buying the book, and a tying up of any loose ends not covered in your summary. Following this you should have "About the Author" and a final page (or pages) listing your previously-published books with their ISBN numbers for your readers to potentially more easily locate them on the Internet. I like to add a few pages of "Testimonials" by professionals/experts whose opinion of me and my book I've solicited for this purpose. Don't worry if you can't get enough of these, even three will do.

You will break up each chapter into sub-titles, at least three, preferably five subtitles within each chapter. Once you get going, you'll discover that you have far more to say, and it won't be difficult to do so. Once you get going, you may find that you have so much material, that you might be able to have enough for a second or even a third or fourth book! (each with different titles and subject-matter.

Here is the most important thing to consider when writing your book: substantiate every point and fact you make from your own or others' clinical research, (credit them if it doesn't come from you) material from your case-book, (remember to change the names and details of your clients) and most importantly, from at least ten books of source-material! You will list at the end of your book your source-material, listing the book-title, author, and date of publication. Remember that writing your book is much like writing a thesis or dissertation towards a specific degree: you'll be essentially arguing your points/case for the readers, working towards a summary of proof. In the "Introduction", state your statement of purpose, or what you will be setting out to do during the course of your book. An example of this is: "For eons, humankind has contemplated the meaning and purpose of life. This book will show how although the meaning and purpose of life varies greatly from person to person, that generally they all agree that the purpose is ultimately to_____ because_____. Remember that the purpose of your book is to back up your points with material from experts in their field so that you ultimately make an air-tight case. You should include at least 20 or more quotations from these experts with citations and references to each quote which includes (in parenthesis) the work's title, and specific page and paragraph, author and name of the publication, even if it's say, Wikipedia. In that case you would supply the url, for example.

You should include a "Discussion" chapter, (do not necessarily call it "Discussion") where you are essentially debating with yourself the points you've made, resulting in ultimately proving your points/evidence.

Getting Your Book Published

You can go about this in many ways.

Self-publishing means you put out the initial expense for the actual publishing of the book; this may or may not include employing someone to correct the grammar and sentence-structure. Then you must have it edited; can you do this yourself, or you may have to pay someone else to do this. "Trimming away the fat" of your book isn't an easy task, as we are seldom completely objective about the whole affair; employing a professional to do this will prove costly, but worth it! You will likely take personal offense to the changes initially made to your "work of art", but believe me, the editor's mandate is to get your book up to a marketable, professional standard, and not to personally attack you. There will also be other expenses once your book is published so that it may be distributed broadly, (both physically, as well as digitally and through social media outlets) and MARKETED, or made to be "needed"/"desired". This is also just as important as writing the actual book!

Getting a major (or even minor) publisher to publish your book is an arduous task, but once (and if) you accomplish this, you are home-free, as they will do all the work for you, including developing and designing a professional and marketable cover art/design, editing, and distribution. If they are "legitimate", they'll not ask you for any initial, "up-front" fees, and only take a percentage of sales; you'll be asked to sign a contract with them for both of your protection; this is all normal. Remember: if they ask you, or keep asking you to pay them, run! Research online, or in books such as "The Writer's Market", a list of LEGITIMATE, big-city publishers, most of which you've likely already heard of, (such as Simon & Shuster) and find out what they want to see, as far as standards, theme of the material, content, etc. Then, send them ONLY a SAMPLE of your manuscript, either digitally or as a hard-copy, again, whatever they request, along with an introductory letter/cover letter. When I was starting out as a professional cartoonist (the process for getting your cartoons published in newspapers and magazines is similar, except you must approach comic-strip SYNDICATORS, as opposed to PUBLISHERS; believe me, I had HUNDREDS of reject-letters, but I persisted until I finally hit/succeeded, ironically within my own home-city of Montreal with a local, major syndicate and newspaper! I never looked back; PERSISTENCE PAYS!

Publishing on demand sometimes requires that you pay an up-front fee for the services, but the whole thing is WORTH it! Much better than self-publishing and sitting on a room, garage, or warehouse full of books! Just look up "Publish on Demand" on the Internet, and GO for it! Remember, "buyer beware", as some will charge more outrageous fees than others and ALWAYS try to "Up-Charge", (charge you for more "necessary" services) but with publish-on-demand, you are more or less at their mercy, especially if you can't edit your own work, or design the cover-art: they will charge you upwards of a thousand dollars for each of these services! But they WILL distribute your books widely, and print them up as needed, hence "print-on-demand": you can request (and pay for) only what you think you'll need, for example, for a book-signing or book-launch. If you only need a couple of dozen books, you pay for them, (with your author's discount) and they'll send you that, after all of the initial costs, design, editing, etc. fees.

I HIGHLY recommend you go through Amazon's publishing services, as they are "print-on-demand", but they'll charge you NO upfront fees, only your "author's fee" (wholesale, 25% of the retail price of the book) for as many hard-copies as you require: no sitting on thousands of books, only (say) a dozen or so for your event, at a discount! They'll also put your book on their Amazon website so that you can sell it that way. They also offer Kindle publishing services so that your book can also be published as a Kindle, (also advertised at no cost to you, on their site) one, or the other or both hardcover and Kindle. All for free, as they only take a small percentage of sales! Here's their url:

https://kdp.amazon.com/en_US/help/topic/G202059560

Good luck, enjoy writing, and remember to write because you ENJOY it, not JUST because you want to make a buck from it. Remember that you either have a TALENT for writing, or you DON'T, just like you either HAVE a natural TALENT for DRAWING and/or PAINTING, ACTING, SINGING, PLAYING a musical instrument, etc., or you DON'T. All the technical training in the world won't make you a BETTER artist, just a more TECHINCALLY PROFICIENT one. You can either play, write, etc, from the HEART, or you CAN'T. Your audience will absolutely KNOW the difference, and so will your potential booking agents. You're either a natural-born ENTERTAINER, or you're NOT; your audiences will know for sure!

Seminars/Speaking/Workshops/Sunday Morning Gatherings

The combination of creating an image of yourself in the public's eye as an expert in your field by writing your book and having "legitimacy" in the form of university degrees should seal the deal! This should make you "desirable" in the eyes of agents as a speaker and lecturer, and thereby commanding a higher, professional fee.

This is where you want to be in relation to your professional career, and it often takes several things to achieve being a speaker, or lecturer. It's easier to merely hold workshops, be they "certification" workshops or otherwise. Here's why.

In order for you to be desirable in the eyes of an agent to book you for speaking engagements for corporations and major organizations, (you WILL require an agent to do this, as it looks more professional, and the organizations/corporations often have scores of agents that they EXCLUSIVELY deal with for these purposes; it's just EASIER for them) you must have the YEARS of both working in your field, have AT LEAST one or more books published, and most importantly, already have years of having ALREADY been booked for years of speaking engagements! It's the age-old problem that novices face, straight out of college or university: the companies want experienced professionals to hire, and yet they often won't give a beginner a break! How do you get your first speaking "gig", so-to-speak? Just keep sending out your promo-material and credits, (academic as well as professional) and EVENTUALLY you WILL come to the attention of an agent who will give you a "break", usually at a much lower fee than more experienced speakers. Don't get discouraged, just carry on with your career, keep writing, do your private practice, see your clients, and promote yourself widely on social-media with inspirational memes and videos. (More on producing podcasts and webcasts later) It is all a "building process" towards your ultimate goals, be they writing/publishing books, public speaking, producing podcasts/webcasts, etc. You can also be content to be the BEST therapist/practitioner that you can be, helping scores of others to help themselves and building up your practice.

Suppose, however, that you are required by law (this varies from state-to-state and Canadian province-to-province) to do a Sunday morning service, gathering, etc. to maintain your metaphysical license and title as "Rev. so-and-so". This is often the case if you've earned your degree online through a legitimate seminary school, such as the University of Sedona and University of Metaphysics' *International Metaphysical Ministry*.
(https://internationalmetaphysicalministry.com)

Let's say that you don't feel comfortable doing public speaking. What if you have no previous experience in this field? This means that you won't be pursuing public speaking, for one thing, and that's alright, there are plenty of other vocations within the metaphysical field to pursue, such as achieving various credentials in modalities including Reiki, Prana healing, Hypnotherapy, teaching meditation, Qi Gong, Tai Chi, Yoga, etc. etc. But you'll still have to fulfill the legal obligations required to keep your metaphysical license by holding a Sunday morning service, either weekly or once-a-month. How will you do this? How will you come up with the necessary (and hopefully thought-provoking) topics and overall structure of the presentation? It will have to be AT LEAST an hour in length. Will you have LIVE or RECORDED music?

First thing's first: either get acting lessons, (including movement and speaking/projecting) and/or certainly attend as many Toastmasters meetings as you can, until you feel comfortable speaking in front of a crowd!

This will help you overcome your shyness for public speaking, and you might even find in time that you wish to do more of it! That covers the speaking part of your ministry/Sunday morning gatherings/service, but what about topics? You can gather topics from problems and issues in everyday living, and certainly from the University where you got your degrees, certainly at the very least the topic of your Thesis and Dissertation is a good start.

Dig a little, Google "Metaphysical Topics" and do your research, and soon you'll have enough topics for a few gatherings, maybe more; once you get the momentum going, more ideas will come. You might find that in time you'll be able to use your Intuition as far as the following week's topic should be! It will likely be more relevant than you realize, and that SOMEBODY in the crowd will benefit from it. Make sure that you quote (during the course of your lectures/Sunday topics) from an "authority", be it someone famous in the metaphysical/self-help field or otherwise, from your own book, and/or from any one of already-established spiritual texts. This will help you to "hammer home" your points.

As far as live or recorded music is concerned, if you sing and/or play an instrument, you can do this yourself, gathering some of your inspirational songs that you might have already been singing and playing. Borrow some from Sunday school, for example, the songs are pretty (pardon the pun) UNIVERSAL.

If you have musician friends who are willing to regularly add their talents to your gatherings, enlist them for the task! If worse comes to worse, you can use recorded music, which although not as dynamic in feel and nature, will accomplish the purpose of getting people up and participating at least with their voices and energy, and breaking things up as far as your format is concerned.

As far as I'm concerned, getting two meditations to share at the beginning and at the end of your service is just as crucial as choosing your topic. This and the take-home program is all-important, as it will leave them with a promo of your presentations, as well as points and structure of what they just saw, so that they'll more easily remember what they saw. It also makes for a great souvenir. Remember to charge them a "donation stuff-money-in-the-donation-box" type of entrance fee, in other words, "By Donation". I found that if you have a shoe-box sort of affair with a slit in it, with "Tithing" or "Donations" written or printed on the box, is sufficient; put this on a table near the front of the room or entrance to the room, with your promo-material, brochures, books, etc, nearby/beside it. Have someone in charge of taking any monies, at the beginning and end of the service, especially for the books, CD's, DVD's, etc. which you might have for sale.

Acquire your two, five-minute meditations either from the educational institution where you got your degrees, and/or Google "Affirmative Prayers" or "Affirmative Meditations" and use them, as long as they're copyright-free, especially if someone is recording the proceedings and posts it on social media! You don't want to get into any legal problems, especially as a metaphysical minister!

I recommend using classical music behind your spoken words, as it will make everything more meditative as you speak the words of the meditation. If you can find Mystical/Higher Consciousness Meditations scripts online, even better, just be sure to speak them softly, but not so softly that the recorded, classical music drowns you out.

We've covered your Sunday morning service/gatherings/presentations, and following are ideas for your programs. The following was from my own handouts.

First, the front and the back of the handouts…

(Back)

Opening Affirmative-Prayer

Here you would have an affirmative-prayer/positive statement which you read line-by-line and have your congregation repeat.

I recommend anything by Ernest Holmes.

Closing Affirmative-Prayer

Here you would have an affirmative-prayer/positive statement which you read.

I recommend anything by Ernest Holmes.

Have your contact information at the bottom of the page...

www.drmichaellikey.com
(778) 232.2155
dr.likey@gmail.com
The ISLC is a registered, non-profit
incorporated society

(Front)

Celebrating Life!

(Logo)

Address/Location of Service

The inside may include an original song (as indicated) or a standard, up-beat hymn…

You Can Do Anything You Want
(Theme-song for the TV-show "Magic Mike's Castle")

-Dr. Michael Likey-
© All Rights Reserved ACAP/SOCAN/BMI

La...La...La...La...La...La...

You can do anything you want, be anything you please,
See anything you want, do anything with ease!

There is magic in the air,
Moon-dust everywhere!
Close your eyes and you'll see,
Open them and believe!

You can do anything you want, be anything you please,
See anything you want, do anything with ease!

Opportunities are wide,
Look there, deep inside!
And soon you will see,
All will come to be!

You can do anything you want, be anything you please,
See anything you want, do anything with ease!

La...La...La...La...La...La...

An Actual Program (Suggestion Only)...

Spiritual Mind/Soul Science and Psychology
Dr. Likey's The Science of the Soul:
"Scientific-Prayer-The How's and Why's"

Spiritual Treatments/Scientific-Prayer/Affirmative-Prayer/Spiritual Mind-Treatment- All the same term for re-training, altering, eliminating negative thought-patterns and attitudes, using meditation/self-hypnosis, plus visualization, emotional, and mental discipline.

Why *Scientific*-Prayer?- Because: (A) Concrete proof/results have been noted as a result of clinical study and observation of many cases. (B) There are definite steps, again after numerous testing, those proven to be the correct steps and order.

Results/Proof- Have included altering of unwanted attitudes, thoughts, beliefs, and lifestyles of the patients in the studies. Also "demonstrations"/"materializations"/"manifesting" of physical results such as increased income, and improved health.

Meditation/Self-Hypnosis-Altered-state, to provide a susceptibility/suggestibility of the patient for planting new and healthier attitudes deep into their sub-conscious.

Scientific Prayer-The method for planting the new and healthier attitudes. Comprised of *Unifying/Identifying*, *Denying*, *Accepting* (declaration/affirmation of positivity, as if it is already so), and final "stamp": *And So It Is!*

Here is the general structure of my Sunday morning gatherings, which, by the way, is also the general structure of my live presentations and lectures!

Somebody might read aloud the "Opening Affirmative-Prayer Treatment" (for example) or some other meditation, for example, from Ernest Holmes, which the audience follows along/reads aloud from within the program.

- **Introduction (Who I am, my credits, etc. What we are going to achieve with this presentation)** (5-minutes)

- **First song. (Original, and from one of my CD's)** (3 minutes)

- **Higher Consciousness Meditation** (5 minutes)

- **Lecture (They can follow along with the points made in the handouts/program) Note: I might use a white-board, or Power Point, to hammer home the points I make in the lecture)** (Approximately 40 minutes)

- **Second Song (Might be original, or could also be a famous one)** (3 minutes)

- **Higher Consciousness Meditation** (5 minutes)

Someone might read aloud the "Closing Affirmative-Prayer Treatment", or something from Ernest Holmes, again, which the audience will follow along/read aloud, from their program.

NOTE: This is for suggestion only. Please follow your own structure, which will make the service/gathering more original.

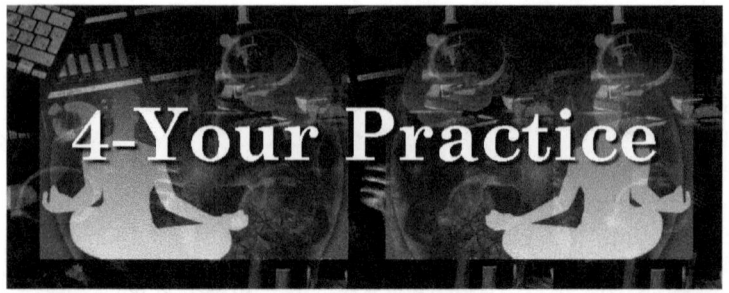

4-Your Practice

Once you are adept at, and have earned your certification at the very least, let alone done several "readings", hypnotized others, etc. and have gained experience in whichever modality or modalities you are equipped to practice, (hypnotherapy, for example, or perhaps it is astrology, palmistry, psychic readings, the tarot, Reiki, Prana Healing,) then you must decide where you wish to start your formal practice, in order to charge a fee.

Do you wish to keep it a home-based business, and have your clients come over to see you? You will save a lot of money on rent and other expenses you may incur as a result of leasing office-space, including insurance, electricity, phone, book-keeping, etc. It is certainly cheaper to work from home, but it is also less professional, unless you have ser up a formal room/office in your home for this purpose. What about book-keeping? Are you able to do your own, or should you hire your own accountant to keep all your books, taxes, etc. up-to-date? You must consider this, as well as the other expenses previously referred-to. Regardless, let's say you have set up office-space in your home or in a commercial space; what will the décor reflect?

If your business is more New Age, then you may want to decorate with pictures on the wall of nature, lotuses, people meditating, etc. You may have New Age music playing in the background, and have silk pillows on the floor and bamboo curtains and dividers, like a 1960's "hippy" abode. You might even have incense burning, or some subtle scent and lit candles. This is perfect if you're offering astrology, meditation classes, palmistry, and/or tarot readings. Alternatively, you might have a more business-like, sterile environment, especially if you conduct hypnotherapy there. It all depends: who are you, and what would you like your environment to reflect? I for one went with a bit of a combination of both scenarios, since I offered all of the above services, plus workshops and classes.

Your fee is something very important to consider as well.

You must charge whatever the going rate for any of your services is, despite the lack of experience you might have; you never want to be accused of under-cutting others in order to get business. More on this shortly.

Also remember to pay extra (when leasing space or using your home) for insurance, again, you don't want to be slapped with a malpractice suit, or worse, for sexual harassment, touching, etc. Consult with your insurance broker about these concerns and how to be covered for them.

Following is information from my book, *The Powerful Healing Gift of Prana*, (ISBN: 9781074017194) available from Amazon. It is in regards to you conducting business as an energy-healer, or Metaphysical Practitioner, which you will find crucial.

By definition, a Metaphysical Practitioner uses energy to facilitate the self-healing of their patients and clients using either hands-on methodology, and/or absent, or distant healing, as outlines earlier. The healing energy may include Reiki, Ling Chi, Prana, or Chi (Qi). The particular system of healing employed by the practitioner may include the system of Reiki, (outlined in detail in my paperback books on Amazon: *Master Reiki*, (**ISBN-10:** 1515026248 and **ISBN-13:** 978-1515026242) and *Master Reiki, The Dissertation.* (**ISBN-10:** 1985025515 and **ISBN-13:** 978-1985025516) The Prana Healing system, (outlined in detail in this book) is another system, as is the system of Qi Gong Healing.

(**https://en.wikipedia.org/wiki/Qigong**) In fact, we included earlier as well, a healing modality/system from New Thought philosophy, referred-to as "Affirmative", or "Scientific Prayer", wherein the Higher Mind within both the client and the practitioner connect, (Spiritual E.S.P.?) and the practitioner sends positive changes/outcomes with faith, conviction, and belief, resulting in the eventual physical materialization/healing/wholeness with the hoped-for result since it "originated" in the Mind of the Universe/Higher Mind!. We can also refer to its origins/category as being Spiritual Mind-Science or Theocentric Psychology. The "cousin" of Spiritual Mind-Science is Science of Mind, originated by Ernest Holmes.

Whichever system and energy you employ, the fact is that you are considered to be grouped under the general title of "Metaphysical Practitioner". Other terms are "Spiritual Healer", as well as "Energy /Energetic Healer" and "Spiritual Energy Healer", etc. Whichever title you choose to group yourself under, the fact remains that you are also an "Alternative Wellness Practitioner" who employs "complimentary medicine". You may refer to your treatments as a "Metaphysical Consultation".

It is crucial that when promoting/advertising your services, you must provide a disclaimer stating something to the effect that "healing and medicine are two very different disciplines: therefore, Reiki (or what services you provide) is not medicine but healing, and does not constitute medical advice. In case of serious illness consult the practitioner of your choice, preferably a competent health care professional." This should cover you legally, in that you are out-rightly stating that you are not a medical doctor, nor do you profess to be, nor do you practice conventional medicine, and in fact that you encourage everyone to seek out professional medical advice. It is also important to include in your disclaimer that "everyone responds differently to your services, and that there is no guarantee of success, nor the degree of success. The client/patient approaches your services at their own risk."

More Legalities

Because you will mostly deal with physical issues/conditions, and you are working (mostly) one-on-one with your patient, it is crucial that they sign a waiver prior to any treatments that you may provide, stating that they understand the difference between medicine and healing (as outlined previously) and that there is no guarantee of success. When providing healings at religious/metaphysical gatherings and services where others are present, this is not necessary, as long as they are aware that everything you provide is at their own risk, with success not guaranteed. Always ask permission first before laying hands/making physical contact with the client/patient whether you are in public (gatherings) and certainly in your private practice; maybe even include the fact that they give you permission to make physical contact during the healing, in the waiver!

Never try to diagnose the physical condition, or you may be accused of practicing medicine without a license. You can provide instead "karmic", spiritual, and/or emotional reasons.

Never prescribe any kind of medication, not even aspirin; even if the item is non-prescription, you could be accused of practicing medicine without a license.

When laying on of hands in private during treatments, (with permission first) be careful that the treatments in no way resemble any kind of physical manipulation, or you can be accused of practicing chiropractic or osteopathic medicine without a license. Laying on of hands is considered acceptable before a spiritual audience, but can be considered legally suspect when done in private.

Be extremely cautious if anything you do in your healing practice resembles healing "equipment" of any kind. As a Metaphysical Practitioner you should never imply that any machine is doing the actual healing.

Remember that holding a Sunday service with others present provides legitimate reinforcement in the eyes of the spiritual public, as opposed to any potential legal problems you may incur in a private practice; as much as you can, do your healings in public, with an audience present. Remember to first get a legitimate Metaphysical Practitioner's license, which gives you the legal right to hold your services and to provide healings. The University of Metaphysics (with their parent seminary school, The International Metaphysical Ministry) is a great start: https://internationalmetaphysicalministry.com

Educating the Client/Patient

Educating the client that initially approaches you to help with their situation/ailment, etc. is crucial, as they must know all of their options. Hopefully you have more than one modality, or system, to offer them, so that you may tackle a wider range of issues. Many times a potential patient approached me wanting Reiki (for example) to alleviate their ailment; I suggested another modality that I am also qualified to provide, Hypnotherapy, for example, because I believed it would have longer-lasting results. A thorough explanation of what they can expect with the particular modality/system is crucial as well, so that they are less apprehensive about it all, and also get an education in the process.

The more knowledge the client has, the better; they might even be able to practice something on their own at home, if applicable, for example, self-hypnosis. I almost always give my patients "homework" to take away with them, (for example, a list of positive self-esteem affirmations) or one of my affirmative/life-affirming audio-CD's for them to listen to, so that they might build their confidence/self-esteem/worthiness. I take a few minutes after our formal session to teach them, for example, how to take themselves into an altered-state of consciousness using self-hypnosis or meditation, and then listening to the CD, or planting their own affirmations within their subconscious by saying over and over (while in altered-state) the written affirmations.

Regardless, the more education you provide as to how Spiritual Mind-Science Healings work, the more faith they will have in it working, and therefore the more effective will be the healings, as they, with faith, will become more receptive to allowing the self-healing to occur!

It is crucial to let your patient know that the amount of time for them to heal varies from person-to-person, but that the healing you provided will continue to work over several days. Some healings are instantaneous; others take minutes, hours, days, or weeks. Sometimes your patient will call and tell you that they actually feel worse because of the treatment! You must inform them that this is part of the process, and the ailment must first "come to a head" before they'll get better/notice any positive results. Reassure them that even if they felt nothing during the treatment, it is still working, that the healing energies are so subtle, they may not feel anything; the same goes for distant/absent healings/treatments.

I highly recommend that you tell them all of this first, before starting a treatment.

Let them know that with Hypnotherapy, for example, they may not think that they are "under", that being semi-conscious/awake during the process is normal, and that the suggestions go deeply into their subconscious regardless.

Educate, educate, educate, then heal, heal, heal!

Fees

The best advice I can give you at this point is to find out what the going rate for a Reiki, Prana, or any kind of energy-healing session is in your area, and go with that. It may be a rate based on the full hour, or any part of that hour. The energy-healing session may be only one part of the entire Metaphysical Session/Consultation, which may include an Intuitive Reading, Astrology, Theocentric Psychology, Meditation/Hypnosis or anything else within the hour/half-hour offered, in which case you must go with whatever the going rate for a Metaphysical Consultation/Session, again, in your area/region is. Don't be concerned that you are just starting out; you may be tempted to charge less/undercut the other professionals who were working at it for many years, but don't...you'll build resentment in the eyes of the other professionals if you do, and thus limit how many referrals you might have received from your peers! Besides, it's just not fair, as your lower prices may attract to you (and perhaps away from those charging more) more clients/patients than if you were charging the going rate. Resist the temptation to undercut as a result of lack of confidence, or worse, bad business practice!

Note as well that prices for metaphysical sessions vary widely across the country, and in larger-populated regions the fees charged will be definitely higher than say in the smaller-to-midsize markets. For example, in the smaller-to-midsize market in which I reside, (and considering that I've been doing it locally for twenty-five years) my fee for the hour is $200. This fee includes a one-hour session of two Higher Consciousness (five-minutes each) Meditations, an Intuitive and Theocentric Psychology/Spiritual Mind-Science/Eastern Psychology session, as well as either Reiki, Prana, (for physical ailments) and a Meditative Mind-Treatment, (re-programming the client's attitude employing Hypnosis/Meditation to a Higher Conscious state.) for their emotional and spiritual well-being. I know that it sounds as if they're getting a lot for their money (and they are) but keep in mind my sessions rarely go for an hour, they usually extend into a second hour! (total two-hours) So they are actually paying $100. an hour, as opposed to my advertized $200. an hour. The reason for this is that the client may only require the one hour (in which case I get my $200.) which might only include the Intuitive session, with a bit of Reiki, for example; with other clients, they may require more modalities than I've listed, and go for an hour (or even two!) extra, for a total of two-to-three hours, greatly reducing my fee! (I still receive the $220.) Don't limit yourself or your clients, (while being fair to yourself) and give them what they need! Start off with the advertised fee of (say) $200. for the hour, and see as you go along if they require more time. Another way is to offer a fee-structure of (say) $200. for the first hour, then $100. each hour thereafter. Again, go with what the local rates are and don't under-price yourself!

Up-Front Fees, or Not?

Another important consideration is whether or not to offer pre-payment, or "fee up front" or not?

I recently had a client whose wallet suddenly "disappeared" mysteriously once the session was over, and I had just finished writing a receipt for payment for them. This was their first visit with me, and I had already done my "screening" process with them. (more on that later) the result being that I determined that they had no major psychiatric/psychological issues and therefore my sessions would be well-received and successful in their eyes. I trusted that they would pay me when I asked them for it. I always ask for cash-basis payment (I declare everything for the "tax-man" for my workshops and sessions, except when I'm hired either through an agent or a larger corporation, in which case we use either PayPal, Direct Payment, credit-card, or worse-case scenario, check) and have immaculate and up-to-date book-keeping. They asked me to follow them downstairs to their vehicle, because they were fairly sure that their wallet fell out of their purse and is lying somewhere on or near the front passenger-seat of their truck. As we approached her truck, my mind started racing, resentfully reaching negative and judgmental conclusions, after all, I gave her a three-hour session! As it turned out, her change-purse had fallen into a receptacle in her side passenger-door, as she believed! The lesson learned for me was: don't necessarily jump to negative conclusions, and to ask for pre-payment, even for the metaphysical sessions, which previously I did not; the client would always pay me in cash once the session was over.

What if the Client Cancels?

You've booked a session with so-and-so (with their phone-number and e-mail) into your schedule book, either hardcopy and/or virtual. You receive a message either that day or the previous day that they must cancel, and they'll contact you when they're ready to re-schedule; (this usually means they've backed out for whatever reason and you're not likely to see them) sometimes they'll ask to re-schedule with you, in which case they're likely sincere and you will see them down the road.

Regardless, you didn't ask for pre-payment; you also didn't let them know (and through your promotional material, website, etc.) that you require minimum 24 hours cancellation notice otherwise part or whole of their fee (up to you) is non-refundable. Just think: that was potential income you could have received! How do you insure that you receive full, or part of your fee? The answer is simple: get full payment up-front, (as previously discussed) and let them know, either in writing (e-mail) and/or verbally (don't trust that they've read your entire website) that you require minimum 24-48 hours notice of cancellation, lest you keep 30% of the deposit/your fee. If they're not okay with this, and they've promised to pay you after, you shouldn't take them on as a client or workshop attendee, something is wrong, and its not your problem. Another thing that I've heard from potential clients/workshop attendees is "I can't afford the fee; would you accept a smaller amount?" My answer to them is, "Just come back (or register) when you can afford it, no problem!" Say this lightly (as if there is no problem, nor judgment) and don't look back! Trust me, no one ever got ahead with a "sliding-scale". Some practitioners use a sliding-scale based on the client/student's income/ability to pay because they believe it's more compassionate; some practitioners think it's better to receive part of their fee than nothing at all, but I don't ascribe to this belief. Don't try to offer potential clients/students "two for one" "deals" or "packages", again, honor yourself and what you have to offer! If you give in once, it will open a door for you to continue compromising yourself. Besides, they will respect you more, and it may cause them to seek out someone else who is more right for them in the end, at a lower rate/fee.

The Screening Process

There are ways to screen your potential (first-time) clients before the session by phone, or actually within the first five-minutes of having started the session. In either situation always ask them, "What do you want out of this session?" Their answer will give you some idea of where they're coming from. Do they answer, "I want to be happy" or some such? If so, forget it! If they answer, "I want to know if so-and-so loves me!" (or "Will I ever find love?" or "Will I ever be rich?") Once again, forget it! These folks are looking only for short-term solutions/reassurance that everything will turn out alright. You want potential clients/patients/students who want to know why/what brought them to where they are now, and for them to take responsibility, perhaps using tools that you provide them to improve/grow/gain a different perspective and Higher Consciousness. Very politely dismiss those who don't qualify for your services (self-help) and move on.

Another technique to use, in person, and actually at the beginning of the session (during the fact-gathering phase) is to offer them the first five-minutes free. (this is assuming they have not pre-paid...shame on you!) Say, "If what I'm saying within the first five minutes makes sense and you agree with it, then we'll continue; if it doesn't, speak up, and we'll stop then and you won't have to pay." This always works! That way you see if you're both for each other or not, after all, everyone has a teacher that resonates with them and vice-versa, until they grow; once they grow (or out-grow their particular issues) they might out-grow their teacher/therapist and have to find a new one! Handling the potential client/student in this way will also help you to avoid ghoing through the full hour (or more!) and then having them refuse to pay. (again..."Pre-Payment", and "Non-Refundable")

How Does One Pay for Non-Tangible Services?

What about fees for "Absent" or "Distant" Healings?
How does one go about determining fees/prices for those, and how can honesty/self-regulation be maintained? In other words that the healer will honor the fee given up-front to them by the client by actually doing the distant healing!

Obviously, when the person is not present, there must be an "honor system", or integrity involved with the entire thing.

This is the only way that the healing will at the very least be executed, but not necessarily have success guaranteed. Remember always to include your disclaimer that states, "Results vary widely from patient-to-patient, therefore we cannot guarantee success", or something to that effect. Make sure that you include this on all of your promotional material, business-cards and website, as well as the waiver they must sign, stating this. Include on all of your material and waiver that it is understood that your treatments are not to be considered "medicine". (as stated before) This keeps your integrity to a maximum.

If someone has pre-paid for you to execute a distant/absent healing for somebody daily, weekly, or monthly (Never more frequently than that, as it's "over-kill") at a specific time, certainly honor this and keep to it! Write it down if you must, to remember to do it.

What do you charge? To be fair to everyone, it should certainly be less than if the patient were present, but no more than half of your regular fee.

If you normally charge a client (in-person) two-hundred dollars an hour (for example) then it's alright to charge the flat rate of one-hundred dollars for unlimited distant/Absent Healings.

I hope this helped to shed some light on fees, and a little bit about business practices and ethics.

Next, we'll cover promotion and advertising.

5-Promotions & Advertising

The following is also from my book, *The Powerful Healing Gift of Prana.*

Let's assume your healing skills have evolved sufficiently that you've been getting outstanding feedback from friends and family; they're saying that what you've predicted has mostly come to be! You're ready to take it to the next level: charging for your services!

Being a professional doesn't only mean charging for your services, it also means being and acting like a professional! Remember to dress as if you're working at a major corporation when going out on jobs. (or "gigs" as some of us call them) Males should be neatly-groomed, with suit and tie; females similar attire, neat and tidy, perhaps a business-suit/blazer.

Our goal here is to change the image that metaphysical/spiritual healers have, from charlatans and "flakes" to working professionals who exude tasteful opulence, from your personal appearance down to the look and feel of your props (if any, such a massage-table, brief-case, incense, incense-holders, candles, music, etc.). It's acceptable if you've found your "character" as well (medieval attire for example) for appropriate events such as psychic fairs, themed events, etc. Remember that you must stand out from the rest, either as a professional, or as your character, as long as you're also being true to yourself; you can't go wrong if you're true to yourself! Always try to stand out from the rest, which you will naturally do if you are projecting an accurate image of yourself.

Why originality is so crucial, is because there is a healer for every client, and a client for every healer! This is actually why psychic and wellness fairs are usually so successful, because each reader or healer appeals unconsciously to a particular age, sex, and demographic. For example, the forty-something male or female will be attracted to a slightly younger reader/healer, (the readers/healers are "mirrors" for the clients) and more often than not, the middle-aged person relates to someone younger, because they like to see themselves as somewhat younger, generally speaking. There are exceptions to the rule of course, but generally speaking, the client wants to be able to relate to the reader/healer, without feeling intimidated, but at the same time, feeling like they have something to learn from them. That's the key: know the demographics of the particular gig you'll be working at! Will it be dressy or casual? Can you provide broad appeal of ages and social status? Can you project an image of upper or middle class? Do you want to appeal to mostly females, or mixed?

Dress accordingly while being true to yourself!

Business cards and brochures/pamphlets are a must! Even simple one-page promos are good. Most importantly, have lots of references/testimonials from clients and sponsors if you can; nothing speaks volumes more about your abilities than word-of-mouth, more so than any advertising can ever buy! Have your brochures and business cards professionally designed, perhaps even with a logo of some kind; nowadays, it's easy to use one's home computer to come up with something that looks truly professional! Make that great impression before the client/sponsor even meets you, with professional and attractive promo material.

Depending on your resources and how serious you are about this all, you might even place an ad in your local newspaper and/or yellow pages; a website and great online presence (including Facebook, Twitter, Instagram, etc.) is also crucial.

Places to Work

House-parties (sometimes called Psychic or Wellness House Parties) where you charge a flat fee for your time and you read as many people as you can within the previously-determined amount of time is one venue; corporate parties, Psychic Fairs, malls, special events and promotions, rural fairs; that's only some of the many places a good card-reader/healer can work at. It's a lot easier to get an agent to book you at larger events, and their relatively small fee (usually a percentage of your gross fee) will make it more than worth it to you. It's easier than collecting your fee/invoicing, dealing with administrative and business details, dealing with the clients, contracts, etc. E-mail out your promo material along with references to as many local agents and party planners as you can, and follow up with a phone call a couple of days later. Follow this same procedure for mall administrators, special event coordinators, and to rural fairs. (all accessible through the Internet) You can also visit coffee-shops for work; they'll let you set up in a corner at a table with a small table-tent sign promoting your readings/healing sessions, or you can go table-to-table offering your services; the same goes for drinking establishments and bars, and clubs. You can see how working without an agent can provide you with more latitude and freedom, but you must collect your fees yourself. (I suggest a contract...always a contract!) You can Google "Contracts" of various kinds and download them. Agents however will do all of the footwork, including collecting the fees; all you need do is have the agent e-mail you your contract, sign it, return it to him/her and show up at the gig; I was spoiled for many years having several agents for my magic-shows, caricature jobs, and tarot gigs, but nothing matched the "thrill of the hunt" in my novice years, hustling jobs, walking into various establishments and showing off what I do, so that they could make a buck from me. That's the bottom-line: show the potential client how they might benefit from hiring you! (why not increase their business by promoting that they have you as a bonus for their patrons, for example)

Generally speaking, if you're working at a coffee-shop or metaphysical store, management/owners will split 60/40 whatever the patron paid you for their reading/healing session; (you can charge the patron $15. for 15-20 minutes for a psychic reading/$100. an hour for a healing) sometimes (as with bars and dance clubs) the owners/management will pay you a flat rate for your time (say 2-3 hours) while you don't charge the patrons, or sometimes they'll pay you a flat rate for your time plus tips from the patrons, for example. Other times the owners/management will charge the patrons a fee for your services, and either give you your amount at the end of the day minus their take (usually 10-20%) or pay you a flat rate for your time. This must be predetermined and settled with a contract between you and the sponsor (management/owners/organizers) before you start any job. You'll have to decide if it's worth it to you to provide the client with a tape or CD of their reading/an audio CD if you do hypnotherapy; this could set you above the rest of your competitors, giving you a marketing edge over others; the store/bar/coffee-shop will love mentioning this bonus to their potential patrons as well! Many readers charge a few cents for their cassettes/CD's or thumb-drive MP3's, but because I like to provide it to my clients as a "bonus", I never charge extra for it.

Sometimes the job will be a one-time thing, sometimes it will be once-a-year if it's a once-a-year promotion/event, and other times it will be a regular (daily/weekly/monthly) gig! Get enough of these and you'll be able to pay a few of your utility bills, or at best, your rent/mortgage or car payment!

Other Services

If you happen to also be quite adept at palmistry, rune readings, astrology, pendulum, etc. you can offer this along with your tarot readings and/or healing sessions, as I did at one time! My sign, promo material, and business cards looked great with all of my services on them, however, it always boiled down to one thing: the tarot or healing: Reiki/Prana/Energy Healing!

I don't know what it is about those services, but knowledge about them and their broad appeal are fairly great, so much so that despite all of my other services, most people chose tarot/healing as their first choice of divinatory tool, Reiki as their healing modality. If they chose a second thing, it was usually palmistry, although seldom.

You can throw in (as a number of other psychics/healers do) a complimentary stone or crystal with every session, providing that you can get them wholesale, and know their general usage.

For awhile (when I had my own kiosk at a public market for several years) I was providing a sheet with illustrations containing the Celtic Cross Spread, with room for me to write the client's selected cards into the relevant spaces, along with the interpretation. This served as a substitute for the cassettes/CD's. I had another sheet with a palm, horoscope wheel, and tarot cards in the three-card spread, again with room for me to write the details onto the sheet for the client, if they wanted more than one service! It was great fun, but all that writing took up too much time and I retired the sheets. Nowadays when I have speaking engagements or lead meditation workshops, I provide (among other things) a sheet with Healing Qi Gong sounds and positions. For awhile as well, when I was studying counseling and psychology, I provided my clients (at my kiosk) with a "Progress Chart" so that they could gauge their own progress in areas of love, money, home, etc. and bring it back to me every three months for another reading/healing and updates to their chart. I even provided a sort of coffee-card at one time: you know the ones that provide you with a free coffee (in my case, a reading) after five paid readings are stamped? All of these commercial attempts failed miserably, but they set me apart from other readers/healers I'm sure!

Developing your E-Mail, Mail, Phone, and Newsletter List

You must develop a phone-call/newsletter/e-mail list of people to inform them of any upcoming events/workshops/seminars/appearances that might be coming up. This gives your business that personal touch, as if you are keeping in touch with your potential, as well as existing patients, clients, and students.

The most effective method is the phone-call list, which gives your business that direct and personal touch, rather than blindly e-mailing (or old-school "snail-mailing") the info out. Continued past experience and practice of phoning people on my list for upcoming psychic fairs/events we'd be holding proved the effectiveness of the calls. We "inherited" the phone-list from the previous organizers of the fairs, and there were well over a thousand names and numbers! No calls were made by the previous organizers in months, so once we got to phoning, many were no longer interested, had moved, or had their phone-numbers disconnected. Thus, the list was whittled-down to approximately 800 people, but a good percentage of people on this list would turn out when called, approximately four times a year. (which was the frequency of our fairs)

But where do you start, and/or continue the list?

We always had (at all of our events) a piece of paper and pen handy, beside the paper, either sitting on the counter, (where people paid for the event) or on the wall. On the paper was the heading, "Wish to Be on Our Newsletter List?" Beneath that were several columns: On the far left, the first column's heading was "Name"; the next column's heading was "Address"; following this was "E-Mail", and the last column's heading was "Phone-Number". Of course, horizontal lines across the page separated the persons' name, etc. so that each page contained room for potentially twenty names, addresses, etc. We always added to our master list from this list at the end of the day, so that we'd have more people to call the next time we held an event.

A Brief Note About The Fairs

I will deviate slightly at this point to elaborate on our fairs.

At first, we were asked to organize the wellness fairs, which were separate from the so-called psychic fairs. The wellness fairs were originated by someone other than the people who organized the psychic fairs, and they also had there own ideas as to how to do it. The wellness fairs were structured more socialistically, that is to say, each of the practitioners equally split the profits at the end of the day, regardless of whether they did ten sessions, or two! This meant that a few, harder-working practitioners "brought in the money", while the other ones sat back and did a couple of treatments all day; this bothered me, because of the obvious unfairness of the situation. I was already organizing the psychic fairs, which had a more capitalistic structure! In that fair, the harder the practitioner worked, the more money they earned at the end of the day. The more readings and sessions they did, the more of a "take" they received. I believe we took 40% of the fee charged for each reading/session, and they received 60%. Everyone was happy with this split. We eventually carried this over to the wellness fairs, and finally merged the two fairs, so that we offered psychic/tarot/rune-stones/palmistry/numerology/channeling/mediumship sessions, as well as Reiki, hypnosis, NLP, etc., etc. This afforded more variety for the client. Sometimes a client would want to see more than one practitioner!

How we controlled the whole thing was thusly: there was no entrance-fee to the fair, and people would enter into the waiting-room area; the event took place in a larger room off of the waiting-room, as well as in several other, smaller rooms, also off of the waiting-area. The waiting-area had several chairs for people to sit while they awaited their turn; we had some snacks/finger-food here, as well as coffee and cold beverages. On the counter were ten or so, smaller, approximately 5"x7" pieces of paper, one for each practitioner. These pieces of paper were taped to the counter-top so they didn't move around, while people signed their name on one of ten lines beneath the practitioner's name. Before they were allowed to sign their name, they paid us the fee of $25. per practitioner, in cash only. This cash-basis made it easier for us to pay the practitioner at the end of the day their cut, and for us to do the paperwork/accounting. The fee included tax, which we paid to the government at the end of the day; I kept immaculate tax-books. If a person wanted to "peek in" and "check out" a new practitioner seated in the lager room, we allowed it, but one of us usually accompanied them, as in the past, many tried to get their readings or sessions for free, lying to the practitioner/psychic, claiming they already paid once they walked into the room. We always kept an eye on people who walked in the door, while we were busy signing up line-ups of people. We eventually made up a larger sign, with Polaroid pictures of the practitioners and their names posted on the wall of the waiting room, and finally replaced that with just the Polaroid pictures of each practitioner taped next to their individual 5'x7' sign-up sheet.

At the end of the day, once the practitioners received their payment, we were left with approximately $350. in our pocket, and out of that, we paid the rent for the space, (The Oasis Wellness Centre, above Reflections Books in Coquitlam, Canada) plus expenses for the food and snacks, and themed decorations for each fair. We considered this a successful endeavor, but it was only successful because of the calling-list, and the work we put into making the 800 or so phone-calls, inviting potential customers to the fair.

Always remember the calling-list.

Next successful, and certainly way less effective than the phone-calls, were contacting potential customers through their e-mail addresses, which I tried previous to one of our fairs as a marketing experiment! This was a total disaster, and we incurred a loss; this is how I can vouch for the successful results of the phone-calls as opposed to the e-mail notifications/newsletters! We hardly had any attendance that weekend to one of the fairs, but it was worth it, so that I could share this information with you.

Other methods of "getting the word out", is through things like "Eventbrite". Eventbrite's advertising claims that "Eventbrite is a global platform for live experiences that allows anyone to create, share, find and attend events that fuel their passions and enrich their lives." In reality, it is an online way (one of several) to organize and generate and take ticket-sales. It is professional for pre-sales, but I offer pre-sale tickets directly, through my own e-mail address indicated on my posters and handouts, as well as my website and virtual/online newsletter. I like having more control that way. Another way to solicit potential clients and customers for your events is through online social marketing groups like "Meet Up". I have tried this, both by paying their fee, as well as their free version, again, with little practical results; sure, it's fun building an online "community", and sharing information and like-minded friendships, but again, for physical and actual dollar-sales, nothing beats the direct-contact phone-call list. This goes for Instagram, Twitter, Facebook, LinkedIn, and other social media methods: they're fun for gathering friends and maybe even potential business contacts, but again, nothing beats the "real thing", the human contact and phone-call list: either they're serious about spending, or they're not!

A few words here about business meet-up groups, of which several of my compeers indulge in. These meetings occur (usually) in board-rooms, and much sharing of business techniques, marketing, etc. (maybe even potential business?) goes on. Often there's a fee to join; sometimes there's snack you pay (or not) for. This is today's "networking", but let me ask you, who really benefits from this? The ones who organize it and take your fee, or you? This is akin to the old newspaper-ad scam, suggesting (in their advertising) that you will "get rich quick" by paying their fee and getting their book/recipe/pamphlet for "success". What it ends up being is a book or pamphlet explaining how to place a newspaper ad offering the same thing! What the reality is, is you are really get rich through people's greed, or their thinking that there's a "magic formula" for richness and success; just follow their same procedure of placing an ad in the paper, offering them information on how to get rich quick, and them supplying them with the same pamphlets/method/formula, and you'll get rich! You can also offer these brochures in bulk, sometimes ordering them wholesale through the ad, but usually by just photocopying the brochure yourself.

There was a trend in the 1990's about supposed "successful" magicians who offered seminars to up-and-coming magicians wishing to get more bookings; there were even books written by magicians with this same theme, which, twenty-five years later, has come full circle and is being offered again! Really, the answer (if you're a magician) is do old-fashioned footwork and cold-calling, knocking on as many doors of businesses as possible, offering your talents, showing them how they can make money by hiring you! That's it! No need to attend expensive marketing seminars on how to do it, just do it! There used to be online ads offering potential customers the same thing, the "key to success" or "successfully marketing yourself". Again, the so-called "experts" teaching you how to get rich, using their formula or formulas, but really, "there's nothing new under the sun", believe me, I've either bought them all, and/or attended all of these seminars! I encourage you to attend them, so that you can observe their sales techniques, but to not get "sucked into" any of them.

That brings us up to this very book, ironically. I claim to teach you how to make a buck from the field of metaphysics, even how to market yourself, to write a book, to hold seminars, etc., and I do that very thing! From making up business cards, to brochures, to online methods and even to social-media networking groups, their pros and cons.

The difference between this book and those get-rich-quick newspaper ads is the intention and experience of the writer! I'm at a place in my life where I've done it all, and my intention is to merely share it with you, not to scam people in order to get ahead! Sure, I can teach you "cold-reading" (fake psychic readings) which I've never done before in my life, but I have a conscience! Instead, I am offering you the fruits of my labors, information and experience worth, by-the-way, infinitely more than the price of this book! I'm thankful that I can do that.

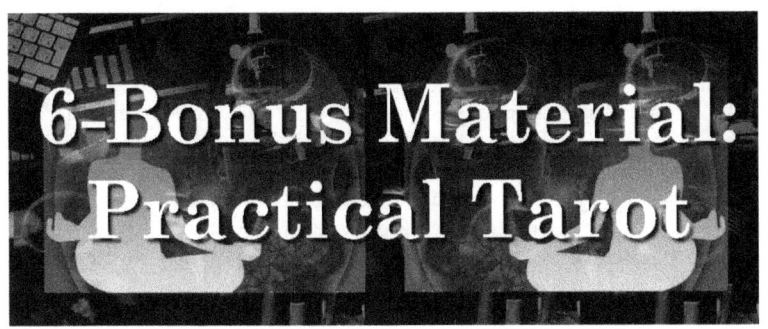

6-Bonus Material: Practical Tarot

At this point, I would like to include some bonus material for you, if-you-will. Essentially, they are my books, *Practical Tarot*, (ISBN: 154840313X), and *Developing Your Psychic Awareness*, (ISBN: 154839968X) both available from Amazon.

Consider them my gifts to you, from myself, for having purchased this book. You will also find them to be very useful, especially if you intend to start a metaphysical/occult/psychic-reading practice. When I would hold seminars and workshops on these themes/topics, these books would be the text-books/manuals that I gave to my students. Consider them to be professional work-books for the student and potential professional, so if you are looking to expand your practice to include psychic/intuitive readings, tarot, or any sort of divination and meditation/self-hypnosis, etc., this will certainly expand your knowledge base and help you a great deal.

Introduction to Practical Tarot

So you want to learn how to read tarot-cards? You're fascinated with the beautiful and eclectic images and imagery; something within you lights up and feels familiar about the cards. It feels right to shuffle them and to hold them in your hands, yet you're still not sure.

You've likely had a past lifetime or three where you used the cards for one reason or another, and here you are today, again faced with these beautiful and historical objects. It's crucial that you understand this: will you use the cards strictly for fun, to occasionally check up on yourself and/or friends and family, much as you might with the daily horoscopes, or are you more serious about it all? If you are serious, you must understand the concept of healer vs. fortune-teller.

A healer facilitates the mental, physical, and spiritual well-being of themselves and others, while a fortune-teller attempts to predict/forecast future events, sometimes using other divinatory tools such as regular playing-cards, runes, pendulum, astrology, etc. Ideally the fortune-teller is also a healer, who might use healing modalities, (such as modern medicine, nursing, psychology, psychiatry, chiropractics, etc.) and/or alternative wellness/holistic practices such as Reiki, Touch-Therapy, etc.

One more thing; rather than "fortune-telling", let's refer to the art of predicting future events as "divination"! Let's attempt to educate the broad public as mush as we can.

There are numerous excellent publications about the tarot, some of them giving you in great detail the occasional fictitious and occasionally accurate history and background/origins of the tarot, meanings and interpretations of the cards. I have taken great care to read as many books on this subject as time permitted, and thus I have included a relatively extensive bibliography at the end of this book.

History

Recently I have discovered that the oldest known images relating to today's tarot can be traced back to 14th-century, hand-painted cards from Egypt. Known as Mamluk cards, after the dynasty of governing sultans descended from Turkish slaves. The game played with these Mamluk cards was known as Mamluk Wanuwwab, or "The Game of Kings".

If we look at regular playing-cards, we can see how tarot-cards are the great-great grandfather of them.

For example, the suits of regular cards (clubs, diamonds, spades, and hearts) evolved from the Minor Arcana's suits of the tarot: batons/staves/staffs/sticks/rods/wands, (clubs),

pentacles/rings/disks/discs, (diamonds) swords/spears, (spades) and cups. (hearts)

In a general way, the meanings of the suits have evolved and maintained the original meanings: Spades: (Swords/Spears) physical action, Hearts: (Cups) love and emotional issues, Diamonds: (Coins/Discs/Rings/Pentacles) money/financial/material/home, and finally Clubs: (Batons, Staves/Staffs/Sticks/Rods/Wands, the unseen/intuition/inner-strength and sometimes business/shrewdness.

The Jacks evolved from Pages and Knights, Kings and Queens, well, from Kings and Queens.

Likewise, the suits of both the tarot and regular playing-cards correspond to the elements, the directions, colors, and the old calendar/ancient celebrations/seasons: **Coins**, (north, winter, green, Dec. 21st/Winter Solstice, earth) **Cups**, (water, west, Autumnal Equinox/Sept. 21st, blue) **Swords**, (east, air, Spring Equinox/March 21st, yellow) **Wands**. (south, fire, Summer Solstice/June 21st, red) Keeping this in mind, one can see how the tarot related to the Celtic Wheel of Life, and thus, a fuller interpretation may be given.

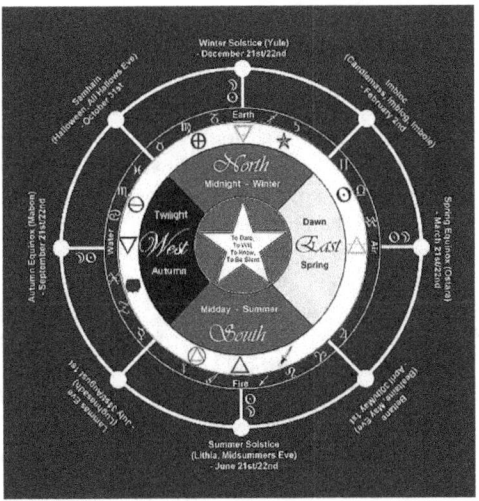

The tarot has 78 cards in all, the modern, regular pack of cards has 52. The tarot is divided into two parts (The Major and The Minor Arcana) The Minor Arcana has 56 cards containing the aforementioned four suits along with Pages, Knights, Queens, and Kings, and The Major Arcana has 22 cards starting from "0" (or "The Fool", from which "The Joker" in regular cards has evolved) to "22" or "The World".

Superstitions

One should not buy their own cards, as this might bring "bad luck". Not true, of course, but isn't it nicer to receive from a loved one a tarot-deck? Don't worry, and buy tarot-cards that feel "right", or "speak to you", if-you-will.

You should not read for yourself. Again, pure nonsense, but how objective a reading can you do for yourself? Always better to let someone else read you (preferably a stranger) At the very least, reading for yourself might give the reading a "wis-ful-thinking" slant!

Don't read yourself or someone else more than once a day. Why not? Nothing bad will happen, but often times the exact same cards will come up! Really...I've tried this with myself and dozens of others...the same cards will repeatedly come up in the reading, and if this isn't giving a clear message, I don't know what is!

The cards are evil. Why? Really? Sure, there is much subliminal messages within each deck, but often times this belief/fear comes from people coming from fundamental religious backgrounds. The cards are merely ink and cardboard (objects) and nothing more!

The practice itself of reading cards, and/or divination in general is evil. Again stemming from fundamental religious groups who fabricated untruths during medieval times or earlier for control over the general populace; whatever or whomever didn't follow a particular religious practice or practices were deemed heretics, evil, of the devil, etc. and subject to kangaroo-courts which found the non-practicing party or parties guilty and sentenced to torture and/or death. Part and parcel of these "laws" and beliefs included self-empowering practices such as meditation, certain dances, self-hypnosis, and of course, tarot-cards and divination in general which were "not of God". We should keep superstitious fears and nonsense such as this away from the healing arts and divination; as it is, the broad lay public associates card/tarot readings with con-artists, gypsy fortune-tellers, etc. The less educated the populace, the greater the chance of people moving towards the healing/divinatory arts as opposed to science, but also the more prevalent the prejudices and biases (religious and otherwise) against these practices there will be.

You must cut the cards with your left hand. It's funny how many times I've had clients ask which hand to cut the cards with, or how many times they must cut them before the reading. This ritual, no matter how it is performed, will not affect the accuracy of the reading! I remember shortly after relocating to a smaller center on the west coast of Canada from a larger eastern location in the early 1990's, the fear-filled and superstitious clients would close their eyes, tilting their chin upward, and gingerly cutting the cards, sometimes with trembling hand, or worse, waving their arm over the pack in some arcane ritual before selecting a few cards; I'm not sure what they were thinking, but it was difficult to keep a straight face, holding back laughter from these poor souls! I remember them cocking their heads and listening intensely to every word I spoke, to insure that they would not miss a word I uttered, as if their entire life hinged upon the slightest word or nuance I expressed!

Now don't get me wrong; ignorance exists everywhere, but I have found that too many people place too much emphasis and power in the hands of a psychic reader and/or the cards, pendulum, etc. The cards, runes, pendulum, etc. are merely a tool, a means to an end! I, and I'm sure any reader worth their salt, could read using a sugar packet, or a pencil!

It's not the objects, but the reader! It's not how you cut the cards, it's the reader!

Whether a reader channels their angels, spirit-guides, or even Higher Intelligence, (preferably) they will give an accurate reading either with the cards, no matter how they have been cut or dealt, or with a particular swing of a pendulum. In my book and course *Developing Your Psychic Awareness*, (ISBN-10: 154839968X) I emphasize meditating (preferably Mystical/Contact/Higher Consciousness Meditation) for years before attempting a reading. This is to allow your unconscious mind time to acclimate to God's Higher Frequencies, allowing your Intuition (God-Guidance) to more easily come to the surface of your mind, thus allowing for a more accurate reading. What will further sensitize you to God's energy-factors include Reiki, and any meditative practice, including playing with your tarot deck, as the Higher subliminal messages worked into the pack will assist you in opening your mind to Higher Intelligence, creativity, peace, love, and joy. God, or Perfect Mind will therefore in time come up from the very center and nucleus of your mind to the surface level of your mind, healing your unconscious mind of negative karma and trauma, and allowing you to channel God (if you will) as Intuition.

Cutting the cards with the opposite hand that you write with allows you to use a different part of your brain, as does cutting the deck three times and completing the cuts, again with the opposite hand that you write with; this allows for an easier accessing of your unconscious mind, where memories and visions past, present, and future exist.

Spontaneously cutting of the cards (without thinking) also helps to access your unconscious mind easier, for the same reason. Often times after I "clear the deck" first of any residual unwanted energies, (including previous clients') by shuffling a few times and visualizing (or In-Visioning/Imaging) clean, white-light/God-energy breathing over the cards, I'll place the cards down in one heap, asking the client to cut once without thinking, using the opposite hand that they write with. This method has unfailingly worked for myself and my clients.

No-one else but you should handle the cards. Really? Then how can you get the client's vibe into the cards so that on some level they work for you both?

You must keep your cards wrapped in a silk cloth and stored under your pillow at night. Again, nonsense! Why would you even want to do this? At the very least, you want to keep the cards energetically neutral, and during a reading, have the client put their energy and/or intention into the cards, energetically cleaning them between readings as previously described.

I get it; it's old-school to make the deck your own, and some readers won't even allow others to touch their cards! But you really want to have the client's vibe in the deck for the reading, not your own! So grow up, don't be so possessive, and follow procedures as previously outlined.

Set Ups, Rituals

Let's assume you just received/bought your cards.

Really, you can remove the clear cellophane from the box, remove the extra advertisement-cards and instruction booklet which comes with the deck, and go for it, assuming you know the literal meanings of the cards, before attempting to use your Intuition/Psychic abilities for an interpretation that will be tailor-made to suit your client's intentions, wishes, and questions.

Really!

I guarantee many will disagree with me on this, and that's okay; they're entitled to!

The more experienced you get working with the tarots and other divination tools, and the more sensitive (psychic/Intuitive) you become, you'll begin to notice the difference in feel between a fresh, brand-new deck and a seasoned, well-worn one. You might even begin to prefer the fresh feel of a brand-new deck each time, what with the smell of ink and slick surface; if this is so (and I recommend this regardless) then you should "cleanse"/consecrate the cards before each reading! The theory is that this way there is no energetic residue left over from previous clients. There are numerous ways to do this, some of it depending on your belief system, and how much time you have between readings, and your environment. If you want a completely energetically neutral deck when you first get it, I recommend burning sandalwood or rose incense and/or sage and sweet-grass while placing each card, one at a time, and turning each card over (front-to-back and back-to-front again) a foot or two over the smoke.

If you have Level 2 or Level 3 Reiki, you can positively "re-program" the entire deck's energy field at once by placing the cards between your hands/holding the deck in one palm, while the other palm lays on top of it. Visualize the Reiki symbols going into the pack, while repeating over and over again the corresponding Kotodamas. (Read my book or watch my video of the same name, "Master Reiki", available on Amazon to understand what I just said.)

Personally, I shuffle the deck until it "feels" clear, (if you can't "feel" yet, just shuffle three times) or exhale Chi/Ki (cleansing breath) through your nose (visualizing it as white, pure, God-Light) at the cards while you shuffle them a few times. This will make the cards feel lighter for sure, but again, don't worry if you can't feel yet, merely follow these procedures; in time you will become more and more sensitive, and you will begin to "feel" energy. Time-wise this works for me, especially if I have several readings lined up. To further save time, once I've cleansed the cards between readings, I ask the querant/client/guest to shuffle the cards three times (to get their energy into the pack, but you need not tell them this is why) and then I ask them to, without them thinking, to spontaneously cut the cards once with the opposite hand that they write with, for the reasons previously outlined. I then proceed either with a full *Celtic-Cross Spread* (I'll explain this later) or a three, six, or nine-card spread. Sometimes I'll use what's called the *Astrology* or *Clock Spread*, consisting of twelve cards dealt out (after the cleansing and clearing rituals) in a clockwise fashion; this will allow you to, after setting the intention to do so silently in your mind, starting with the noon, one, and two-o'clock positioned cards to represent December 31st, January, and February, three, four, and five-o'clock positioned cards to represent March 31st, April, and May, and so forth, all the way around to eleven o'clock, or November, making for quite the extensive, year-ahead reading, best suited as a "New Year" reading, done in late December for clients.

Again, to speed up sensitizing yourself psychically and Intuitively, I recommend the exercises in my book "Developing your Psychic Awareness", available from Amazon. **ISBN-10:** 154839968X **ISBN-13:** 978-1548399689

Box or Cloth?

Again, this is a personal preference, with no occult associations attached to it.

Truth be told, you don't really have to store your cards in an attractive wooden box, or wrapped up in a silk cloth or both. Sure, from a presentational perspective it looks really cool to unwrap your cards from the cloth which you then lay out as a smooth "working surface" for your cards, opulence being the idea here. I actually do this on occasion, especially if I'm working a corporate gig and I don't know what kind of table (if any) I'll have. (make sure they at the very least provide you with a folding card-table if you are working elsewhere other than your home!) A wooden table isn't necessary either, although energetically, wood, in theory, is neutral, and not a conductor (if you will) of any kind of energy; I suspect this is the real reason in the past wooden tables and boxes were preferred. I loved to "play up" the gypsy aspect, done tongue-in-cheek, at some gigs, using a wooden box which houses my silk-wrapped cards, especially if it's a non-corporate event, such as a "psychic house-party". For corporate gigs, I'll dress professionally, jacket, shirt and slacks (like an ad executive) and carry my "close-up stage" in my leather portfolio. I'll remove the "close-up stage" from the portfolio, and then lay it on the provided table, and it looks amazing, with its gold railings and green-felt, padded top. The cards alone (no cloth) may then just be in the wooden box, which I place off to the side, with the cards being the focal-point on the "stage". Presentation is everything! Also, the host and the clients will feel psychologically more accessible with these wonderful surroundings you've provided.

Often times I will also (in addition to the deck) have in my wooden box a pen, a small pad of paper, magnifying-glass, (if I throw in palmistry) an extra set of reading glasses, and the all-important timer, essentially a kitchen-timer which, if loud and distracting, you may keep on the floor at your feet, as long as you and your client hear it go off at the 5, 10, or 20-minute designation, allowing you enough time to read everyone at the event/party. I also keep business cards in the box as well as in my pocket. I used to use a hand-held tape-recorder, and at the end of each reading provide the client with a 30-minute recording of their reading; I printed up my logo and glued a special label on each tape, placing it in the cassette-case, which also had my custom logo/graphics on an insert. Sometimes I would throw in a business card with the cassette as well! Of course, I always had several extra cassettes on hand, and an extra hand-held recorder and batteries, just in case of emergency, especially during crazy-busy psychic fairs! In the last few years, WHEN I provided recordings of the readings, I would supply it on a custom-printed CD (again, my logo printed on it), utilizing my laptop (which I would bring along) to record and burn it onto the CD, which took all of a couple of minutes…plenty of time to "schmooze" the client or sponsor. I was thinking of recording the readings onto a thumb-drive, (really very accessible and inexpensive at this point; I must credit this idea to the gifted Runes man Richard Hanson) but at this point I no longer provide recordings; the clients may take notes if they want!

Choice of Cards

We might as well discuss this, even though I can't dictate to you your personal preference/taste. The only deck I have an aversion to is the *Thoth* deck, (sometimes referred-to as the Crowley deck) which, while aesthetically beautiful, contains subliminal messages created by its designer, the world's foremost Satanist and cult-leader, Aleister Crowley. I can't recommend this one!

I must, however, recommend the following traditional and historical decks! The *Rider/Waite* deck: Great for both working pros or beginners, this British deck from the 1920's is very "clean" subliminally as well as energetically. The *Carey Yale* deck: From 16th century Milan, Italy, this oversized and gorgeous deck is the grandfather of all tarot decks! Not recommended for beginners as there are no numbers nor type, and there are actually eight extra cards in the deck. Each card is a hand-painted work of art, suitable for framing, which the originals are, in museums in Paris, Milan, and New York! The *Tarot de Marseilles*: originally black-and-white woodcuts from 12th-century France, the current incarnation (in color) evolved from those exact same 12th-century pictures, but were colored from the 17th-century on. Flat and archaic-looking illustrations, they are straight out of history! The *Connolly* deck: From 1970's America, the creator, Eileen Connolly, had her son paint this deck, which is clean and fresh looking! She also penned several tarot workbooks to go with the cards. The *Morgan-Greer* deck: A contemporary deck which feels and looks old, again very nice to work with! The *Aquarian* deck: My very first deck, could be tough for beginners as the images/figures of people are close-up/from the waist up, without to much else going on! I still recommend it, though! The *Universal Waite*: Somebody took the illustrations from the *Rider* deck and re-colored it with softer, pastel colors. Beautiful and somewhat easier on the eyes than the bright, comic-book-like colors of the *Rider/Waite* deck.

All of the aforementioned decks should be available from your local metaphysical/occult store; again, look at their samples and choose which one feels right. There are also many kinds of "Oracle" and "Animal" cards, "Dragon" and "Faery" decks, etc., but I would recommend at first mastering, so-to-speak, the standard tarot cards before you attempt to interpret these deviations; this way the original hidden and standard messages and images of the tarot can go deeply into your subconscious mind, thus allowing an unconscious adapting of them to the deviation-decks.

Home or Office Vs. Portability

When doing readings at home or at your office, choose a nice quiet area, perhaps at an attractive table or desk, with three chairs: one for yourself, one for your client, and one for their friend. I always give my clients the option of bringing with them a friend or family-member who may sit-in on the reading; this puts the client at ease, and who knows? The friend may decide (after witnessing your reading) that they too want one! Some readers won't allow an "audience" during their sessions, which some people don't like or appreciate, after all some friends/family members are protective of their family/friends! Why not encourage an audience, therefore? Besides, from a marketing perspective, this will make you seem more open and welcoming! I myself encourage audiences, as for many years I was a television and stage entertainer; I also had my first big start reading people in a club/discothèque, with loud blaring music and drunks asking me lewd and lascivious questions! This sure helped me to develop my ability to focus in on things, despite a distracting environment! Reading cards at a kiosk in an open market on the west coast of Canada seven-days-a-week, nine-hours-a-day for six years also helped to discipline me and my ability to focus intently on things, again without being distracted. I also developed patience, tolerance, resilience, compassion, and sharpened my sense-of-humor as a result of dealing with the myriad of extremist and abusive fundamentalist groups who daily harassed me! I had never encountered this in the larger centers previously, so there sure was a learning curve here!

If you haven't be fortunate enough to have this sort of experience and background, I wouldn't be surprised if you preferred no audience, watching defensively over your shoulders, so-to-speak, at your home or office!

Speaking of home or office, if you do have the luxury of an office or corner/room of your home, (as opposed to going out to do corporate jobs, house-parties, etc.) then you can determine whether or not you want to have a kind of "New Age" feel, (with incense, candles, pillows, etc.) more spiritual, with pictures of mandalas, Buddha's, nature, along with diffusers, etc., or more professional, with office-space sort of furniture, filing cabinets, etc. Just determine who you really are, and go with it! As long as you provide a quality, comfortable environment for your clients. If you're on the move at house-parties, etc., you can take my previous suggestions about portability and the use of a portfolio or large purse or bag.

With or Without Psychic/Intuitive Ability?

You must decide whether you can read using your psychic/Intuitive abilities or mechanically, initially.

You'll naturally know when you feel more comfortable when practicing on fellow students, family, and/or friends. Do you find yourself rattling off accurate information with little effort? Words just come to you and they flow? You don't hesitate to say whatever comes to mind…in fact, it hardly stays in your head, it just rushes out through your lips? This is where you want to be psychically/Intuitively when reading the tarot for others! If you're not there yet, you can still initially give a good card reading without using you're soon-to-be-developed psychic/Intuitive gifts/skills. In the interim, meditate daily, regularly, and ongoingly; not that western, guided-visualization stuff, but the real thing: Eastern Meditation! This is sometimes referred-to as Higher Consciousness Meditation, or Mystical or Contact Meditation, essentially for the purposes of divine contact. I warn you, though: the real thing has no glamour or glitz, there are no lightening bolts that will hit you! If you're meditating correctly, you'll feel a peace and contentment come over you; this is how you'll know! Increase the amount of time you meditate, over time, for example five minutes at first, eventually ten, then twenty minutes. Twenty minutes twice a day ongoingly is sufficient for "evolving your soul", or developing your psychic abilities/Intuition. Practicing Yoga or T'ai Chi will help; being a Reiki or a Prana practitioner will help as well. But it is only Mystical Meditation that will get you there! Read my book *Developing Your Psychic Awareness* (**ISBN-10:** 154839968X **ISBN-13:** 978-1548399689) in which I go into more depth and include some exercises as well!

There is absolutely nothing wrong with doing tarot readings without using your psychic/Intuitive gifts at first, for family and friends. This will be a great training ground for developing confidence doing readings, but more so, it will help you to remember and to integrate the literal meanings of the cards into each reading. If you plan on making a living from readings and doing them professionally, then you must use your psychic/Intuitive gifts! You must be able to provide (at the very least) specific situations, people, places, and things for your client, and answers, in a detailed manner, to as many questions that they may have for you! You bet I combine the literal meanings of the cards with more specific time-spans, months, years, and descriptions of people, after all, my clients deserve this! If you can eventually do this to any degree after several months of reading, then great, your abilities will likely develop more and more. If you can't do this to any degree, you might want to re-think everything, and just read for family and friends. Again, don't lose heart, and keep meditating!

If you are able to provide with some degree of accuracy some details, do so, but try not to make predictions too far up the road! (I find three months to be the maximum that one can relatively and accurately do this.) Why? Because Higher Intelligence/God is mostly in control, plus we have some degree of free-will; it is with this free-will (and only with this free-will!) that we have some latitude. What I love to do is provide for the client all the future possibilities/scenarios that I see; (usually three or so) one of these is bound to come true! Also, too, remember that readings/future forecasts are like weather forecasts: you might see/hear/feel something coming up in whatever time-frame, but like a weather prognostication, that "high" or "low" headed our way may suddenly (for whatever reasons) blow north, south, east, or west! So it is with psychic/Intuitive tarot readings! I have found (in the past) that the degree of accuracy dropped in relation to how far down the road the reading was, in other words, experiment initially to see how accurate your readings are when predicting or "seeing" three, six, ten months down the road and stick to that. The time-frame may increase in time. Thus, when laying out the cards, you can say this is for three, six, or whatever months down the road.

An Exercise

Let's try doing a three-card spread (which is very good for a standard, five-minute reading) for a friend or family member now. Assuming that you're dealing cards face-down from right-to-left, set the intention in your mind of the far right card being the past, (a base from which the client is coming from) the middle-card is the current situation, (present) and the far left-card, the future. At the same time, set the intention of a time-line for this card; (the future-card) is it three, four, five, or more months down the road? Decide beforehand in your mind and stick to it! Subconsciously you will program your mind to psychically pick up on the information to be had for that particular timeline. Stay confident and sure of yourself when picking up impressions. Time will help you to improve. Just let the words come forth without hesitation; the more you do this, the better you will get at it.

You can also experiment with a six-card spread! Lay out the first three-cards from right-to-left again, (face-down) setting a time-line intention, following with the last three cards, again right-to-left directly beneath the first three cards. The first card is always the past and a base from which the client has built from. The last card is always the future. (again, six months or more down the road? You decide beforehand!) Try to build a story of events (as you turn each card face-up) starting from the first card (the person's past base: happy or abused past, for example) leading to the present set of situations and circumstances, then moving on to the future. You can do it! Just be sure of yourself and tell the story, not allowing the person to interrupt you until the end, upon which time you gather up the cards (so that they can't go back to each and every card asking about it!) and ask them to ask you a specific question, which you will answer for them by them cutting to a card, or a series of cards. Remember questions and answers at the very end, once you've given them the main reading. Don't let them interrupt the flow of what you're saying in the main reading. Then you can relax with a "yes" or "no" cut, for example.

Another Exercise

Here's one straight out of my "Psychic Awareness" workshops; it's fun, easy, and accurate!

Use a regular pack of playing-cards, and remove all of the Jokers and advertisement-cards. Make sure you have a pen/pencil and paper to keep score.

The idea is to intuitively separate the blacks (clubs, spades) from the reds (hearts, diamonds) without looking at the faces of the cards! I have my students pair up, mark their score, and then have the other one of each pair do the dealing. One person deals the cards out (faces down) one-at-a-time, into two piles, while the other person calls out "red" or "black". Use twenty random and shuffled cards for this. The dealer hold up (backs towards the "guesser") each card, the "guesser" says "red" or "black", then each card is placed into the predetermined red or black heap. At the end, one counts up how many red cards were guessed correctly from the red pile, similarly how many black cards were guessed correctly in the black pile. The amount, or score is noted, then the "guesser" becomes the dealer.

Everyone has always scored better than 50% correct, usually on average 70%! Probably because the students already have a higher-than-average degree of E.S.P. (extrasensory perception) At the end of the 7-hour workshop (which includes several meditations) everyone always scores higher than at the beginning of the day, when they do this experiment again, proving that to some degree, they have improved their psychic/Intuitive abilities and that the meditations worked! Use this experiment/exercise and have fun!

"Yes" or "No" Deal

I love this deal, because it's at the very end of the reading, and you can more or less relax, after all, it will give the client a definite "yes" or "no", no arguing there! You don't even need to use your psychic/Intuitive gifts for this!

After doing your main reading, (the three or six-card spread, or even the Celtic Cross Spread…more on this one later!) have the client (in their mind) ask a question that requires a "yes" or "no" answer while shuffling or cutting the cards three times. Taking the pack from them, you then proceed to deal (faces up) into three heaps (from right-to-left) thirteen cards each, unless you get to an ace, in which case you deal that ace down onto the particular heap, and then move onto making the next heap of thirteen cards, or again, unless you reach an ace, dealing onto that pile and moving on to make the next heap. You should be left with three heaps regardless, some might have thirteen cards and no ace, other heaps may have an ace. The point is, if there are three aces faces up, the answer is a definite "yes"! If there are only two aces faces up, it's a pretty good bet that the answer is "yes". If only one or no ace, then "no". Pretty good for not using your psychic/Intuitive gifts, hmm?

Let's move on to the meanings of the cards, and a wonderful spread, broadly accepted for its thoroughness and accuracy, the Celtic Cross Spread.

Here I will give you "thumbnail" interpretations of the cards for easy reference, based on my years of experience with many, many decks. I've found that over time, I noticed specific patterns in relation to the meanings of the cards, but remember too, that the specific meanings may differ from reading-to-reading, just as the players, or clients' lives differ from reading-to-reading.

If you have a poor memory like mine, you'll find these brief interpretations easy to remember, so that you'll have a base of the literal meanings of the cards, allowing you to relax more so that your Intuition/psychic ability can come forth more easily, combining for, and providing the client with, an exceptional reading.

Years ago I designed and successfully sold my own tarot deck. (in two sizes!) Because I choose not to dictate the kind of deck you should use, as well as for brevity, I am not including any illustrations with the explanations: the names of the cards should be enough! Go forth and learn!

The Major Arcana

This is the spiritual journey of the tarot! The Major Arcana consists of 22 cards, starting with 0 (The Fool) and ending at 21. (The World) Generally speaking, the journey starts at naivety/a child who goes through life's trials and tribulations, culminating in success, achievement, etc., only to start all over again, learning and experiencing more through different situations, and culminating in wisdom and experience. The journey starts again, continuing again, and ending once again with more abundance and prosperity. As you have surmised, the endless journey always begins at the beginning, hopefully always at The Fool (0), signifying no loss of faith and hope/seeing through the eyes of a child each time the journey re-begins, and ending in gain/prosperity, and again not losing heart and being cynical and negative!

0 (The Fool)-Childlike faith, innocence.

1 (The Magician)-The miracle-worker/Healer/Someone who can "move mountains".

2 (The High Priestess)-Our pessimistic nature, sometimes realistic, sometimes just plain cynical and negative!

3 (The Empress)-The archetypical "Mother/Earth Goddess".

4 (The Emperor)-Wisdom from life experience, maturity, loss of innocence.

5 (The Hierophant)-Wisdom from spiritual knowledge, experience.

6 (The Lovers)-Romantic commitment, marriage.

7 (The Chariot)-Progress, advancement, sometimes a literal trip.

8 (Justice)-Divine and/or earthly (legal) justice.

9 (The Hermit)-Strength from solitude, alone-ness vs. loneliness. Retiring to one's "cave" to re-group and ponder, then emerging renewed on every level.

10 (Wheel of Fortune)-Karma, usually positive.

11 (Strength)-Patience, compassion.

12 (The Hanged Man)-Spiritual wisdom: "no pain, no gain!" Odin hanging by his foot from a tree-limb.

13 (Death)-Transition, change. Rarely actual death.

14 (Temperance)-Pacing oneself.

15 (The Devil)-An obstacle, either self-caused, or caused by another.

16 (The Tower)-Major changes, upheaval…worse than the "Death" card.

17 (The Star)-A period of good fortune.

18 (The Moon)-Phases, patterns; a period of psychic ability.

19 (The Sun)-Bright new beginnings and good fortune.

20 (Judgment)-Judging oneself harshly; sometimes judging others because of insecurity/jealousy.

21 (The World)-Success, achievement, accomplishment on every level.

The Minor Arcana

Understanding a little numerology and the meanings of the suits (symbols) will greatly assist in interpreting the Minor Arcana section of the tarot; of course, always remember to use your Intuition!

Pages-Beginners, like students. They are always self-doubting. No particular age/sex.

Knights-"Graduate" from being the Page/Student. They're building their particular "skill" (based on the suit of Coins, Staves, Swords, or Cups) and they jump on their horse, moving forward. The horse always carries them, regardless.

Queens/Kings-The "Masters" of their particular suit/field. They are sure and grounded, often at the hub of a wheel with others around them. They have worked for this level of achievement. The difference between Queens and Kings: the King is a master, but is narrow-minded, while the Queen, also a master, is more flexible and will listen to advice. Again, no age or sex in particular is suggested, regardless of whether a Queen or a King shows up.

<u>Swords</u>/Spears-Physical action.

<u>Cups</u>-Love and emotional issues.

<u>Coins/Discs/Rings/Pentacles</u>-Money/financial/material/home.

<u>Batons, Staves/Staffs/Sticks/Rods/Wands</u>-The unseen/intuition/inner-strength and sometimes business/shrewdness.

The suits of the tarot correspond to the elements, the directions, colors, and the old calendar/ancient celebrations/seasons/Celtic Wheel:

Coins, (north, winter, green, Dec. 21st/Winter Solstice, earth) **Cups**,

(water, west, Autumnal Equinox/Sept. 21st, blue)
    Swords, (east, air, Spring Equinox/March 21st, yellow)
    Wands. (south, fire, Summer Solstice/June 21st, red)
    Keeping this in mind, one can see how the tarot relates to the Celtic Wheel of Life, and thus, a fuller interpretation may be given.

Numerology and the Tarot

    Number 1-New starts, new beginnings.
    Number 2-Transitions, unfinished business.
    Number 3-Wholeness, completion, closure, finality.
    Number 4-Stability.
    Number 5-**Number 10**-Generally very positive growth, (especially with **Coins** and **Cups**) but is stressful, and self-blame with **Swords** and **Wands**. Generally 3, 7, 10's are lucky, except with **Swords** and **Wands**.

Examples:

Reading from left-to-right:

Ace of Swords-Taking new action.
The Sun (Le Soleil)-A period of good fortune.
3 of Wands-Trust your Intuition!

    Taking new action during this period of good fortune will have good results; trust your Intuition about the outcome.
    Reading from right-to-left, the meanings of each card remain the same,

however the interpretation/reading/forecast differs):

Your Intuition/psychic ability was always in top-form! Trust what you feel right now, as you have a favorable period of good-fortune right now! Quick, focused, and decisive action is likely!

Note: Always set your intention as the client is shuffling as to whether it feels right to interpret the cards from right-to-left, or from left-to-right.

The Celtic Cross Spread

One of the most trusted, durable, and long-lasting of the tarot spreads, the Celtic Cross Spread has served me and many other tarot readers worldwide for centuries. Enjoy my method!

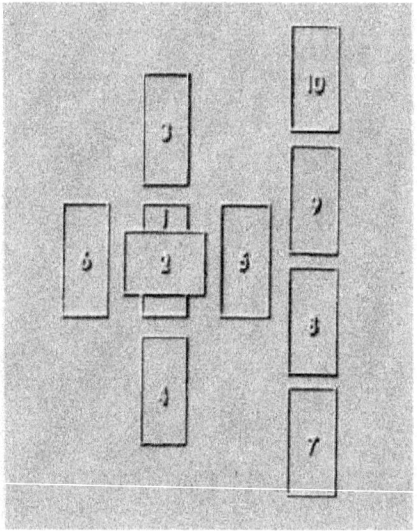

Illustration 1.

After the client cuts the cards, complete the cut and start dealing cards off the top, placing them in the order shown in Illustration 1, faces down.
1-Current situation.
2-What "crosses" the person; an obstacle.
3-This could ultimately happen; distant future.
4-A base they've built from; past.
5-Past.

6-Near future.

7-Reperesents them as well.

8-Environment; physical as well as planetary. (If you're familiar with Astrology)

9-Hopes and fears.

10-Final outcome, like #6.

Turn over groups of cards, as in Illustration 2...

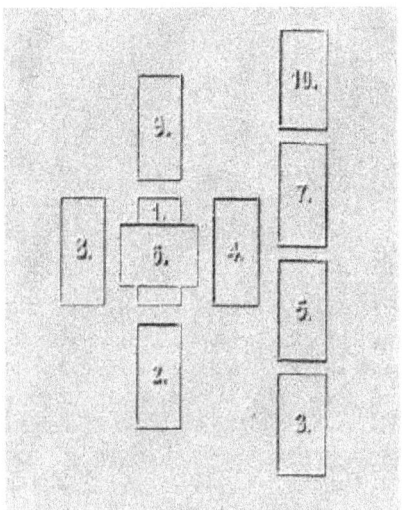

Illustration 2

First, turn over cards #1, 2, and 3. Using the information gleaned from these cards, describe the client's current situation, personality, patterns of behavior, etc.

Turn over card #4, and describe their past.

Next, turn over card #5 and describe any environmental influences such as friends, and family. If you know what's going on planetarily/astrologically, throw that in as well.

Next, turn over cards #6 and 7, to identify any obstacles, hopes and fears of the client.

Finally, cards #8, 9, and 10, which indicate the future: 8 and 10 are immediate future, card #9 is far down the road.

Make sense? I hope so! Now we're going to put it all together for you, doing a sample reading using a spread or two!

Sample 3-Card Spread

Reading from right-to-left:

The client (male or female) is strong and stubborn, with strong Intuition. Their business sense is good, guided by ethical and focused standards. Frequently unyielding to advisors and others often strong-willed and opinionated, the client should always take for granted their uncanny and accurate gut-feeling for business. Currently, there is a positive trend towards changes financially; the client could either go after a job, or a new job/career with success shortly. They should go for any new business ideas or proposals. Shortly, (next three weeks/months) they are in store for big changes; old situations, jobs, etc. could end with new ones beginning. That includes personal as well as professional relationships.

At this point, the client can cut the cards again, and three more cards dealt out in a row (right-to-left) directly beneath the first row, or you can continue dealing three more cards yourself in that order off the top to continue the story/outcome if you think it's appropriate. Remember to use the "Yes or No" spread at the end, and always keep things positive!

Reading from left-to-right:

Major transitions and changes were in the client's past, therefore they are now likely either very flexible and well-adjusted, or inflexible. Regardless, it's a good time to trust one's Intuition in regards to matters of business, and someone (possibly a female) who is a natural leader and very Intuitive, also in regards to business may enter their life in the next while.

At this point, the client can cut the cards again, and three more cards dealt out in a row (left-to-right) directly beneath the first row, or you can continue dealing three more cards yourself in that order off the top to continue the story/outcome if you think it's appropriate. Remember to use the "Yes or No" spread at the end, and always keep things positive!

Sample Celtic Cross Spread

Card in the Center: The Fool
Card Crossing The Fool: Three of Cups
Card to the North: The Hierophant
Card to the South: The Tower
Card to the West: The Lovers
Card to the East: Five of Swords
Cards to Extreme Right, From Bottom-to-Top: The Moon, The World, Queen of Cups, Ace of Swords

Interpret the center-card, southern-card, and bottom-card of vertical-line to the extreme right of the cross first: Opportunity and optimistic trend for the client; extreme changes are in the works in all areas of the client's life, so they might as well go for it/initiate any changes themselves! A trend of strong Intuitive ability should be noted: the client should follow their currently-strong gut instincts, but they should also be aware of any patterns/cycles that they may be prone to right now. (addictive behavior, depression, for example)

Interpret next, the card directly to the east, and the second-card up in the vertical line to the right of the cross: Environmentally and planetarily an incredibly positive trend is indicated; this is a great time to successfully complete a project and/or to take direct action.

Interpret next, the card that crosses The Fool and the third card up in the vertical line to the right of the cross: Issues of love could be present; concerns about an existing and/or former relationship, including control issues, broken relationships, etc. Generally it is positive, though: the person should try to commit to an existing relationship and/or attempt to date more, without fear. They could even attempt to improve an already good existing relationship!

Interpret next the card to the west, north, and the fourth one up in the vertical line to the right of the cross: Near future trends (next three weeks-to-three months) are generally great for love/relationships and taking action in all areas of the person's life; ultimately they will learn spiritual lessons that could lead to wisdom and contentment.

After giving this reading/interpretation using the Celtic Cross Spread, gather up all the cards, cutting and shuffling them to clear the energy, and then you may, at this point, after they shuffle the pack three times, use the "Yes or No" spread for any questions they may have, and remember to always keep things positive!

You can see now how relatively easy it is to give a full reading while you are still developing your psychic/Intuitive ability. Clients always "fill in the blanks" anyway, regardless of whether you use your Intuition or not, much the way a newspaper's Horoscope works: although each astrological reading for each sign is general, people personalize it, filling in the blanks with their own personal details. It is however crucial that you do evolve your psychic/Intuitive gifts if you intend to work professionally, as opposed to for a few friends, students, or family members. It's okay to look up interpretations in a book such as this one if you're reading for friends/family, but it is not okay (and quite unprofessional!) to do this at a corporate event!

Eventually, you will consciously forget the literal interpretations, and because the meanings are now in your subconscious mind, you can go with how the cards "feel" to you, including the colors and shapes.

Feeling the Cards

When you are at this point, you would have done many readings for yourself, friends, family, and/or fellow students/classmates, developing much self-confidence about time frames, spreads, literal meanings, yes or no deals, etc.

Now you can go with the "feel" of a card; look/glance at the colors, the illustrations, the figures in the pictures of the cards, and *don't think*! Just *feel and speak*, not worrying about the accuracy or exact meanings of the cards! How do the cards make you feel? What impressions are they conveying? I guarantee you that you can't go wrong! The cards were designed to subliminally/unconsciously give messages to you. In many cases (especially with the rider/Waite deck) the messages are obvious: a sad figure in the foreground looking mournfully at a spilled cup on the floor; is this person mourning love or what? See what I'm saying? You can't go wrong! Remember to always read the instruction booklet included with your deck, to be fair to the originator's/artist's interpretations.

7-Bonus Material: Developing Your Psychic Awareness

Let's continue, now, with your bonus chapter; this one called *Developing Your Psychic Awareness*.

First off, I want to specify this: Psychic and/or Healing abilities are a gift from God…they are not for our own use, but for the benefit of others. They therefore have a greater purpose: for the betterment of humankind emotionally, physically and spiritually.

More often than not, you'll hear someone ask "If you're psychic, what's my name?" or "If you're psychic, what are the winning lottery numbers?" The average person just doesn't understand (nor do they really have to understand) the reason some of us have been given a "gift", or "gifts". It's really for **them**…not for us to demean a sacred gift/trust by attempting to win the lottery or guess someone's name, but to help them to heal, or to understand why events happen the way they do…for them to know that God, Creator, Higher Power, etc. has control over most events (what some call "destiny")! What is left is our "free will", or the choices we can make based on current and past circumstances and information. Of course, if your belief-system supports this, there's also the short-term influence of the planets (which God created regardless!); the moon draws on the earth's tides, therefore the magnetic-properties of the other planets are believed to draw on us in various ways, not necessarily altering/affecting future/current circumstances, but perhaps at the very least affecting our feelings and emotions on some level or another. For example, pay attention to the days when Astrologers refer to the influence of Mars on the earth…you'll notice you're far more irritable, almost volatile, as are many around you as well; tempers are bound to flair more on those days!

Minor skirmishes are likely to break out in the Middle East during those times, as during the nights of the full-moon (police know this and are out more patrolling on the full-moon nights!)

Pay attention to days when "Mercury is retrograde" (the illusion that

that planet is moving backward, due to it's "loop-de-loop" orbit several times yearly): it's a given that there'll be delays, mechanical things will break or slow down...that sort of thing.

Why the planets affect us in these and many other ways is truly unknown...they just do; believe me, I have more than volumes of data recorded just to see how true this all is.

The sun, too, has been wreaking havoc with communication-devices, satellites and emotions with it's increased solar-flare activity: how can we possibly NOT feel anything when huge waves of flames from the sun occasionally bombard the earth?

The more aware we are of the position of the planets (believe it or not, your local newspaper may actually supply you with enough to go on if the Horoscope column includes a preamble about the overall positioning of the planets before going into each sign's forecast) the more we can at least understand why our spouse snapped at us that day, or why we feel particularly edgy or impatient, or why our car suddenly stalled.

If you have any intention of helping others with your gifts/skills, a general knowledge of how the planets and their positions affect others is crucial. There are numerous resources (the Internet is one) for you to go to for this.

But how do you begin to explore, develop or even discover your gifts?

Altered States

Crucial, as well, to any paranormal/psychic work is the ability to go into an "altered state" whenever/wherever you choose to. This doesn't mean your eyes roll back in a seizure-like grimace, frightening Aunt Zelda and her cat...it's actually like daydreaming! For example, where you "go" when you're bored, or when you have a minute while waiting at the grocery store's checkout...that gentle staring into thin air, if you will. Usually you're looking slightly downward and/or off to the side just with your eyes, and everything goes a little off-focus. Try that now, as you're reading this: allow the book to go out of focus while everything in the background comes into focus (hold the book far enough from yourself so that you can see the pages of the book as well as whatever's behind it, (ie: furniture) allowing everything but the book to be clear); another exercise is to hold a pen/pencil at arm's length, again allowing the pen to go "blurry" while the background becomes sharp/in focus. This technique is also used later in this book for "scanning"/diagnosing/"seeing" any illnesses someone may have.

When entering into a true altered-state (as in Hypnosis), scientists have determined that brain-wave and electrical-output from the brain varies, depending on the level/depth of the altered-state, and they've named each state. The deeper the altered-state, the more the electrical output. BETA is the wide awake state; ALPHA is the next level of depth, and some therapists believe that there are 3 levels of ALPHA: First (great for meditating), Second (good for altering unwanted habits/behavior such as over-eating, smoking, etc.) and Third (good for accessing current past-lives); THETA is the state just before sleeping or just before waking up: this is the desired level for effective use of Hypnotherapy, when the mind is most susceptible/suggestive/open…exploring historical and between past-lives is most easily accomplished here. DELTA-level is sleep.

The ALPHA-state is also excellent for psychic and healing-work.

It has been determined that one can enter quickly and easily into Alpha-state by closing one's eyes, then rolling them up and as far back as they will go without the lids opening. Holding this position for about a minute will induce the Alpha-state, even when subsequently opening your eyes. This explains why in most forms of meditation, the meditator closes their eyes and looks up towards their "third-eye" (the area just above the bridge of the nose) focusing on their breath.

Hypnosis or Meditation?

There are differences between hypnosis/self-hypnosis and meditation, although the brainwave level is the same.

More often than not, meditation is practiced to connect with the Divine (God) and/or for relaxation stress-management.…this, depending on the particular Religion/spiritual practice may include chanting, singing, and/or reading a "sacred" text; it may merely mean sitting quietly on one's knees, or on a chair, mat, in the "Lotus" (crossed-legged) or "Semi-Lotus" position, with eyes opened or closed, focused on a spot just in front and down, listening to one's breathing, encouraging breath deep down into the lower abdomen, focusing up into the third-eye, etc. Often reciting a "mantra" (sacred series of Sanskrit/Hindu-based words) over and over aloud or silently is done. A pleasant scent (such as incense, potpourri, oils, etc.) and background sounds/music may be played as part of the ritual accompanying meditation. Meditation is often done during Yoga, or Tai Chi. It is also a way to focus away from "outside" influences, essentially, and to focus within, where the Divine resides. Various experiences may result, such as seeing light, hearing "music" and/or tasting something sweet.

The additional benefits of meditation are increased sensitivity/psychic awareness and development.

I highly recommend that rather than read "how to meditate" books, you seek out a teacher/yogi/Master to show you how to actually do it. I was blessed to have an East-Indian Mahatma ("Holy-Person") teach me my 4 meditation techniques back in 1989...this was one of the events in my life which subsequently changed everything for me! I was already quite psychic (having inherited the gift from my mum), but the techniques took my on the spiritual/healing path I am still on to this day.

Hypnosis can be practiced on your own (through books and teachers) and/or with a qualified and certified Hypnotherapist. It's benefits are numerous, including practical things such as breaking unhealthy habits; you can explore current past-lives for therapeutic purposes, and your historical past-lives, both for entertainment as well as knowing yourself better. You can rid yourself of fears/phobias, as well as develop better self-esteem and self-confidence with it. You can also treat more serious psychological conditions by addressing issues from childhood, for example.

In short, it is an excellent way to easily and safely access your unconscious mind. Mostly everyone can be hypnotized to some degree (ie-into early Alpha-states), only a small percentage can enter into deeper Alpha and Theta-states, although there exists "light and sound" devices that can apparently take you to deeper levels of relaxation (Theta state). Regardless, any level of Hypnosis will be effective for our purposes of accessing/developing/exploring your healing and psychic abilities.

Guided Visualizations

With the help of a competent Hypnotherapist, over time, you'll be able to access/enter into altered-states by yourself at will. Because seeing a Hypnotherapist on-going can be a costly venture, buying "relaxation" tapes/cd's are highly recommended, particularly those which include not only music and nature-sounds, but guided-imagery/visualizations...in fact, that's all you really need: the guided visualizations that will take you to a deeper level of relaxation, where you can "go on a journey" to meet your angels, spirit-guides, even explore your past-lives and potential future-lives! You really cannot fail with this method; the more you listen to this kind of cd/tape, the deeper you'll go each time and experience more. Don't worry that it's your imagination at work with what you'll see and experience...an hypnotic-state allows you to by-pass creativity/imagination and allows you to go straight to your unconscious, where reality, not fantasy exists.

This was the purpose of the included cd: a "bonus" if you will, a tool, to allow yourself to go deeper each time you listen to it into your past-lives, or to meet your angels/spirit-guides and begin/continue your true psychic/spiritual journey. Think of it as "training-wheels", and in very little time you will have developed your visualization, meditative and concentration-skills so that you can more quickly and easily access your altered-state for healing and psychic-work.

Healer or Psychic?

Believe it or not, there is a difference; the difference is partially determined by your intent, the rest was pre-determined based on what gifts/abilities Creator gave you. For example, you may have been given the ability to "see" more (clairvoyance); you can use this gift to do psychic-readings (with or without divination-tools such as Tarot-cards, pendulum, etc....more on that later) or perhaps God has given you the ability to "see" a particular physical ailment someone has, so that either you or someone else can help them. The ideal situation, of course, is that you use your gifts to help your client, whether it is through divination or actually healing them directly.

I have found it considerably easier to merely ask my guides, or Spirit-Guides for information to help my clients, regardless of whether I'm doing psychic-readings (with or without Tarot), Psychotherapy, Hypnotherapy, Mediumship, Past-Life work and/or Reiki. Because I had been doing hundreds of thousands of readings for 13 years up to that point and Reiki (more on that later), it was somewhat easier to receive answers after merely asking God (prayed for, put out the question/intent) to meet my guides more than 2 years ago. I was already aware of a quiet "sentinel"-figure around me (a protector, tall and hooded figure named Zeseus, pronounced "Hay-zoos") who's purpose was to physically, emotionally and spiritually protect me. I was awakened early one morning by a non-threatening, humorous spirit-entity with dark, short curly hair, slightly over-weight, with possible middle-eastern roots; his name is Hamman (pronounced with a hard "ch" like "chutzpah": "Chah-mahn"). He gives me much information for my clients, and with a decided sarcastic and humorous slant, some of which I must "edit" out...for example, a client's "poor fashion-sense" comment is hardly relevant nor beneficial for them! He is, however, always right on all other matters! He predicts the client's near future (3 months hence), and tells me about their past, giving me precise details including names, dates, places....I tape all readings, because I always forget what I'm repeating from the spirit-entities or guides, that way my clients have a taped-record of their reading to take home. They always return later to confirm all the information. I'm very grateful that my guides are present...they not only make my readings more accurate, but easier for me as well! They even interject with corrections and more information on any "dearly-departed" (more on that later) that I may be doing Mediumship for. Lana is my third guide and introduced herself to me at the same time Hamman did. She has light brown/auburn-hair in a dated 60's hair-do, with a medium-to-heavy frame, short in height. She helps give me a female perspective.

Obviously I'm very "pro" spirit-guides, as meeting them is one of the other things that changed my life and the way I do readings...I can't say enough about the importance of you meeting yours! The enclosed cd/tape is a great way to do this. Don't worry, of course, if you don't meet your guides right away as you're listening to the recording...the more you listen to the dc/tape, the easier it will be for you to enter an altered-state (which will heighten your intuition anyways) and therefore meet your guides. You may go to sleep or wake up to them introducing themselves (as I did), or you may meet them while listening to the recording; in any case, be patient.

Psychic or Intuitive?

While we're talking about intuition, let's distinguish between intuition and psychic ability.

Generally speaking, intuition is "gut-feeling"...it comes from **inside** of you. Psychic ability is generally external...it comes from **outside** of you. For example, your guides are outside of you, giving you information; you are using external objects (such as Tarot-cards or pendulum) to access psychic information; ghosts, angels, spirits, dearly-departed, past-life visions, psychometry, distant-viewing, and other paranormal psychic-phenomena are all on the outside of you (where you want them to stay). Later we'll discuss some more psychic phenomena.

How do you determine whether what you are seeing, hearing or feeling is accurate?

I highly recommend prayer and/or a visualization prior to doing any kind of reading.

Specifically, visualize white-light surrounding you coming from within you and around you. This creates a protective "film" of sorts from people's and entity's negative energy, feelings or "vibes" (vibrations)...after all, who needs to feel all the negativity from an unhealthy client or entity? Secondly (and just as important) do what I call a "rebuking": this is a kind of Christian-prayer that really works, and believe me, you don't have to follow the Christian faith to have it work...I know, because I'm Jewish! The commonly accepted phrase to say in your mind is "I rebuke thee in the name of Jesus!" This will deter any negative/dark forces and keep them "at bay", kind of like a crucifix keeps a vampire at bay. More importantly, when your clients have entities, dearly-departed, "angels", etc. around them, rebuking them is a great way for you to determine if they're "of the light" or not...I've seen too many "tricksters-entities" giving false information, posing as the real thing until they're rebuked, upon which time they immediately shrink down to nothingness and vanish. Trust me...this really works and is something you must do along with the white-light visualization before you start a reading, with the client(s) present…just get into the habit of doing it every time.

Clearing Your Space

While we're on the topic of purification, rebuking and cleansing, let's talk about "clearing your space"!

Basically this is done to the area/space where you do your readings/meditation/psychic-work to keep it light, free of dark energies/entities. You have a number of options, among them: buying cd's/tapes for this purpose…my favorite is called "Sounds of Light" by Crystal Voices, and it's sounds raise the vibration in the area it is played…essentially it is the sound of crystal-bowls being played and they sound like electronic-hums getting louder and softer. It's 45-minutes in length and is by far the most effective, and cleanest way to clear a space. Other methods include burning Sandalwood incense or Frankincense (a resin you put onto a small, lit, concave charcoal-disc which rests in a small pot called a "smudge-pot"…it smells awful but works! Sweet-grass looks like braided pale grass, but burning it smells terrific and it works. In some Native American traditions, another natural product called Sage (while burning, it smells heavy like marijuana) and it supposedly "takes out" negativity, then burning sweet-grass "puts in" goodness and light. Personally, I find sweet-grass incredibly effective during psychic attack (more on this later). Finally, one of the Level 2 Reiki-symbols is used for clearing space and is very practical: all it requires is that you draw it in the air above doors, windows, in corners and other places where negative-energy congregates.

Clearing your immediate space should not be confused with "house-clearing" (or "ghost-busting", if you will…removing unwanted negative energies or entities, which is a far more complex affair and is best left to experts on the subject, as occasionally the entities may pose somewhat of a more physical threat and must be dealt with differently).

Ghosts and Spirits

There is a difference between ghosts and spirits: generally-speaking, ghosts don't know they're dead, while spirit-entities have "crossed-over."

Ghosts seem to exist on a plain/level of existence/parallel universe separate from ours, yet there also seems to be "inconsistencies" within the walls/separations in that, like our ozone-layer, appear to have openings/holes through which things can pass. This explains why/how we sometimes see ghosts who appear to go about their "life," almost unaware of our existence; I suspect that they too, accidentally sometimes see us going about our lives when those holes reveal us to them...just as in a movie that came out several years ago called "The Others" with Nicole Kidman starring...this was a very accurate representation of ghost-phenomena. Conversely, the malicious entities portrayed in movies, throwing about objects and furniture are usually spirits. Spirits know that they've left their "host-bodies" and are free-floating. They can be spirit-guides for the living (either hovering around former family members from this and/or previous lifetimes, sharing their "wisdom"...a note: they still retain the same biases as when they were living...they don't know more than God, don't necessarily accurately predict the future, but certainly confirm things like the nature of their death and may provide closure for the living. Usually they can go at will between various family-members thereby providing insight with a more varied perspective. Those spirits who are "earth-bound" are "stuck" around a particular family-member until they are freed, usually with the assistance of a psychic helping the living-person they're around with closure. See case history in other section.

Spirits can also be somewhat malicious, crusty and irritable, especially if they've existed in spirit-form for years in and around a particular home which has recently been inhabited...to them, it may seem like an invasion of privacy! Sometimes they'll not be angry, but merely want to be acknowledged, and will move objects about to get your attention, or even in a playful manner.

The spirits I mostly deal with I refer to as the "dearly-departed": family-members of my clients who have come to me so that I might repeat what I hear them say, if they actually are around the client. (Sometimes they are not, in which case there's nothing I can do.) I can also see and feel them. The farther away in time that they've passed away or "crossed over", the more transparent they appear to me, and the harder they are to hear.

Some people possess the ability to see, hear or feel the intangible, dearly-departed, spirit-guides, ghosts, etc. This is called clairvoyant, clairaudient and clairsentient. Not everyone possesses all three gifts, however some individuals who have an above-average ability of extrasensory perception (e.s.p. or psychic ability) can do things like see future events in their dreams (precognition/premonitions), move objects with their mind (telekinesis), see people/events/places from a distance ie-different country (distant viewing), communicate with the dearly-departed (mediumship), communicate by having entities speak through them (channeling), leave their body and explore other locations (astral projection), see people's auras (aura-reading), or even their past-lives. I will elaborate on some of these phenomena elsewhere in this book, including some examples from my own case-files.

There are some who organize séances where the Medium communicates with the dearly-departed, and even physical manifestations may occur (like objects moving, noises like voices, moaning, thumps, knocking) or even an appearance in spirit-form of the deceased person may occur. At the turn of the last century in England and the U.S. fraudulent Mediums were bilking the vulnerable, desperate, naïve and often grieving parties out of their money by conducting mostly fake séances, where the manifestations were so fantastic (ie- the dearly-departed may physically manifest out of a thick fluid which apparently emanated from the Medium's mouth!) that the famous American magician Houdini set about to publicly disprove and expose these criminal charlatans. Houdini (disguised) attended numerous séances in an attempt to communicate with his deceased mother, to no avail. He then decided to demonstrate as a part of his stage-shows the same tricks of the fraudulent mediums, thus exposing their trickery. It is thanks to him that people are far less naïve in the areas of psychic phenomena, but unfortunately it has also reflected somewhat negatively on the legitimate psychics. Perhaps in a future volume we will publish ways to determine whether the psychic you intend to see is the real thing or not. Houdini arranged with his wife Bess that after his death, she would attend séances in an attempt to contact him; they had arranged a secret word that he would utter should the manifestation actually be him. After 20 years of attempting to contact him, Bess Houdini gave up. It was never proven that any psychic could contact the great Houdini.

Some magicians after Houdini have included a segment in their shows exposing fraudulent mediums…in fact, it was a "trend" in the '70's for aging magicians, needing a "gimmick" to inject life into their own shows and careers to do this. This is good and bad today, obviously: it promotes a healthy dose of skepticism against the fakes, but it also provides a "sounding board" for extreme religious zealots to speak out against the "evil" doings of the psychics who apparently are doing anti-biblical acts by doing psychic readings. Fortunately, most of the public is relatively educated and can decide for themselves whether they want to visit a psychic and for what purpose entertainment or something more, etc.

In the following chapter, we will explore practical exercises and applications of your own possible psychic abilities, as well as visiting more phenomena and actual examples from my case files.

Psychic Phenomena

In the previous chapter, we explored definitions and differences between altered states, hypnosis, healers, psychics, intuition, ghosts and spirits. Methods of clearing your space were also provided. We also touched on some psychic phenomena.

Here we will go into greater detail of various psychic phenomena, determine through guided meditations/visualizations/hypnosis who your guides are, which psychic gifts you possess, as well as explore the Tarot, pendulum and Reiki.

Reiki

Reiki directly translated from Japanese to English means "sacred energy", not "Universal Life-Force Energy" as has been previously published in most other books.

It is not my purpose to clarify and rectify the myths and mistruths perpetuated in publications as recent as a year ago about Reiki, by well intentioned, but less-read Reiki-Masters.

You can find accurate information in my own courses and books, which have been carefully researched and researched again about Traditional Japanese Reiki; most of the information has been supplied by 100-year-old former students and family-members of the originator, Mikao Usui, and in turn passed on to us.

What is Reiki?

The formal system of Reiki was developed by Mikao Usui, a Tendai Buddhist teacher of esoterics at the request of the Japanese army for paramedic use on their ships during the second world war.

He had been teaching this "Usui Do" (way of Usui) for about 20 years, when after the urging of one of his students, (Eguchi) Usui began to include "Teate" (palm/hand-healing) as part of the curriculum. Likely word of Usui's teachings and healings plus the fact that he had been previously working for the government in numerous capacities resulted in the Naval contract. It is likely, too, that Usui's famous manual was devised at that time to provide practical reference material both for the Naval officers and Usui's students.   Shortly after receiving the Naval contract, Usui opened a number of Reiki clinics throughout Japan, and apparently treated many of the victims of the great Japanese earthquake around that same time as well. About two years after that, Mikao Usui (or "Usui-sensai" or teacher) passed away, it is believed from a stroke in 1926.

Much of the system of Reiki was developed from Usui's esoteric Buddhist   beliefs,   including   the   required empowerment/attunement/initiation ("Reiju" in Japanese) given by the "Shihan" (Master or teacher) in order for the student to be able to channel and transmit the healing Reiki energy to others. This is one of the many ways Reiki differs from other forms of energy-healing: **it is a tradition** (passed on with an empowerment). Other ways Reiki is unique: it has esoteric symbols included in the middle-level of learning it, the Reiki knows where to go without consciously having to control or will it where to go, it can do no harm, the Practitioner cannot pick up any of the illnesses of the clients they are treating, it can also work at the auric-level of the patient, without direct physical contact being made.

There are many other differences.

The reason I'm including Reiki in this book is because it is increases substantially, once you receive a Reiki empowerment, your psychic abilities! It also allows your own healing to begin, first at the physical level, then the mental/emotional level, and finally at the spiritual level. Once you receive an initiation into Reiki, not only do you yourself begin healing on many levels, but you yourself become a healer, as you begin to channel the Reiki yourself.

Even if you don't want to use your psychic abilities to heal others, receiving an initiation into Reiki will increase your abilities psychically; if you intend to help others to heal, then obviously Reiki is for you as you'll begin to do that for others as well after the initiation.

You can see, then, that I'm a great promoter of Reiki, and that I highly recommend it for everyone. If you wish to learn more about it, or even study it through me, e-mail me: **dr.likey@gmail.com**

Beginning Your Journey

Although many of you reading this book have already begun your journey, let's formally get you on your way meditation.

If you have purchased a version of this book that includes some guided-meditations, great! I whole-heartedly encourage you to listen to them over and over so that you can easily get into an altered-state, crucial for doing psychic-work; part of this experience may result in you discovering who your spirit-guides are (more on this shortly); if one of the guided meditations also includes exploring past lifetimes, even better: everyone has had up to, if not more than, at least 23 previous lifetime (or reincarnations), so you'll likely be busy with the recording doing a lot of self-discovery. Knowing who you were in past lifetimes helps you to understand why you behave the way you do, who and why certain people in your life have come and gone, and perhaps what karmic-debts you may be paying this time round as a result of what you did in previous lifetimes. Connecting with your spirit guides will enable you to help others: they will give you information on various things that your family, friends and clients may be seeking. Even if you can already do mediumship, they will offer more details than perhaps the particular dearly-departed may be providing. Always remember to first clear your space/smudge before doing psychic work of any kind and do your rebuking to confirm that any entities, guides, dearly-departed that appear are "of the light". If you've practiced the exercises under "Altered States" in the previous chapter, all the better.

The last chapter of this section, regardless, includes a "script" that you can read and record, then listen to, so that you may enter into an altered state more easily each time, and thus reap the previously-mentioned rewards.

So begin by smudging, finding a comfortable chair/bed, surrounding yourself with white-light and then listening to the recording (either included with the book, or recorded by yourself); I recommend that you use headphones, but merely listening through your sound-system should be just as effective. You can also have a pleasant scent present if you wish and/or dim the lights; remember this is **your** time...your quality time of self-discovery and possibly healing. If you've been practicing and/or have been meditating already for some time, are exceptionally creative and/or have good visualization-skills, you should have results right away...but remember: do not have any specific expectations! These expectations will actually hinder any results. Just "go with the flow", don't expect to be in any big "trance" (you'll actually be conscious and aware of everything going on around you) but be "open"/open-minded.

I also suggest you initially listen only to the first track; leave the past-life exploration for another day! Allow your mind to integrate the new experiences you will have over time. Then when you feel ready, listen to the next track. But enjoy each track for their uniqueness and specialness; in this way you will reap the biggest rewards over time.

Everything we cover from this point on will be from the assumption that you've gone through the recording, regardless of the results, and that hopefully you have a better idea of your life's purpose as well, and are perhaps helping others through the use of your guides.

Clairaudient, Clairsentient or Clairvoyant?

Based on the material covered in the previous chapter, you may have already discovered if you have the gift of clairvoyance, clairaudience, clairsentience or combinations of them. It's not your imagination. If you believe you can see, hear and/or feel more than what's tangibly there, you probably can...don't allow other's skepticism to discourage you...this is your journey. In fact, the way most professional readers do their readings is without doubt: repeating what they can see, hear or feel without stopping to think about it. We just DO it. Any hesitation actually hinders the flow or process; if we worried that others would think we're crazy, or that the information is inaccurate, we couldn't do it. That's the secret…confidence.

Exercise I

I want you to do a "reality check" right now.

Take a regular pack of playing-cards and shuffle them well…make sure that they are in a completely random order. Now, without looking at the faces (or front) of the cards, decide which cards are the black ones (Spades and Clubs) and which are the red cards (Hearts and Diamonds); just place, with the faces down, the cards you believe are red in one stack, and the ones you believe are the black ones in another heap.

Don't think about it…just DO it. This will accomplish a number of things.

First, it will get you to be somewhat spontaneous, and this spontaneity is crucial for accessing your unconscious mind…remember…don't think, just DO. Don't worry what your score will be after the exercise, because I know you'll surprise yourself. All my students do. Go through the pile that was supposed to be all red cards, and place aside the errors…do the same with the supposed black pile, adding these errors to the just cast-aside errors heap.

Count how many cards (errors) are in this pile.

I'm willing to bet that it's less than 26 (or half) the deck. Probably WAY less than 26, and that's pretty good. Imagine: you succeeded by more than 60% in intuitively separating the deck into red and black cards! I've had many students score 75% or more…it's not unusual considering you're taking this course and supposedly possess some degree of psychic/e.s.p. ability! Record this score somewhere, dating it as well. By the end of this book, take the test again…I'm positive you'll score higher. Take the test again in a month, and guess what? Just remember: be spontaneous and don't think. Just DO it.

Exercise II

Now let's get you started on the great-grandfather of regular playing cards: yes, the Tarot! If you don't already have a deck, go out and buy one. Later on we cover Tarot-cards in more detail, including how to buy them…you can look ahead to that section now if you want. Go by the "feel" of the cards: what do the colors/illustrations **feel** like? Do you like the illustrations better in one deck over the other? Do the cards **feel** differently in your hands than another Tarot deck? Take this into account when buying your deck, but **don't think too much!** Go by your initial impression. Once you have your deck, get to "know" them. Read the little booklet that came with the deck; read the history of that particular deck...look at the instruction booklet again, then put it aside. Remove the cellophane wrap from the cards, and thoroughly shuffle them; I mean **over and over!**

Put as much of your "vibe" or energy into the cards by shuffling them over and over again. Don't worry...they're made to be shuffled for years. Now look at the faces of each and every card...you need not study them...just casually go through each card, taking in the overall colors, feel and style of the deck. Enjoy them. They're your "training wheels". Your subconscious mind will absorb the imagery in the cards. If you want, you can find a nice cloth to wrap them in, and/or an attractive wooden box to store them in. There's no superstitious nonsense regarding this ritual...it's merely to have you feel "good" about your new cards. Now set them aside. You've just programmed yourself unconsciously to relate to the imagery in the cards.

Mediumship and Channeling

How many people really know the difference between these two gifts/abilities? I've even met people who do readings for a living but still don't know the difference, which is simple but important. With Mediumship, you are the "go-between" between the dearly-departed and the client. It is you who repeats and describes what the deceased relative is saying, what they look like, or what they are symbolically showing you. *NOTE*: For some reason, occasionally the beloved who have crossed over may "speak" (literally) in a flowery, symbolic almost poetic way; other times they may show you scenes that are symbolic rather than literal (ie- an old baseball glove, cap(with a specific logo/insignia) and ball shown to me in my mind was once the way a client's deceased son "proved"/confirmed that it was him: I merely mentioned that I was being shown those objects and described them, when the client began weeping: she had given her son those very same objects years before. This is how the dearly-departed often make themselves known.

Again, it's important when seeing, hearing and/or feeling the deceased that you don't hesitate...just describe, repeat what they are saying or showing you. Ask them (mentally or aloud) if they have something to tell your client, ask your client if they have questions for their deceased relative.

If you can, ask your guides to confirm any information (they may do so regardless) if you can handle hearing/seeing information from multi-sources simultaneously; I do it, but it's stressful!

Channeling is a whole other thing.

Essentially, it's allowing an entity/spirit/energy into you, upon which time you proceed to speak/act somewhat differently as the entity uses your body to make itself heard. I have done this on a number of occasions, but there are many things to be aware of in regards to channeling. First, does this entity have anything useful to say? Do a double-check first by rebuking and white-light protection. If they're still there, at least you know they're of the light. When I first started channeling regularly a specific entity, I physically didn't feel well; apparently my body was adjusting to the different vibrational-rate of the entity who I occasionally allowed in. Because the information given wasn't particularly interesting nor useful to others, I decided to stop doing this. Channeling, if you can do it, is a personal thing…if you can do it, do it, especially if the information is important. If you can channel someone's dearly-departed as opposed to being the go-between (Medium), go for it. Just remember be spontaneous, protect yourself beforehand and then go for it. Obviously if you have spiritual and/or religious issues about channeling, you may want to avoid it altogether, even if it is easy for you to do.

Psychic Attack/Psychic "Interference"

Occasionally you may experience feelings of anxiety, volatility, irrational thoughts and bickering with family-members, feelings of worthlessness and desperation, anything even physically uncomfortable out of the ordinary. Barring any planetary influences and/or emotional issues, you are likely under psychic attack from someone envious or jealous of you.

It's not the same as "putting a curse" on you…no one can do that (at least not for any great length of time without God and/or your guides and angels intervening); it is the result, sometimes from **unconscious** ill-intent on the part of someone you know…they may not even be consciously trying to affect you!

It is usually accomplished by someone with a high degree of e.s.p. or psychic ability. It always helps to identify them while it's occurring…things seem to stop suddenly for some reason using that method. How? Ask your guides if and who is doing this…have them show you who it is, and the bad feelings will go away almost immediately. If they insist on regularly doing this to you, follow the methods in the previous chapter for "Clearing Your Space"…I find burning sweet-grass particularly effective during a psychic attack. Remember to pray for whomever has done this…always send healing and blessings to those who don't wish well for you…it's good karma!

More Psychic Phenomena

Basically if you are experiencing anything out of the "ordinary" involving "second-sight" such as you seeing, hearing or feeling more than the average person, (ie-Distant Viewing where you can see people, places and events from a distance, seeing people's auras, past-lives, Telekenesis, Precognition, seeing Premonitions, etc.) likely you are experiencing some sort of psychic phenomena because you possess an extraordinary or above-average amount of extrasensory perception; either you can do these things, or you can't! If there are "ghostly" or spirit-type manifestations and you can see, hear or feel them, same thing and same reason, unless, of course average people around you are experiencing the same thing, in which case the spirits or ghosts are demanding attention from everyone and allowing others to see them. It's really not all that confusing, although you must learn to distinguish fact from imagination: rebuke, rebuke, rebuke! If the experiences remain, you are seeing accurately and things of the light (or "good", not evil or "dark"). Of course, some psychic ability/phenomena can be developed, especially those involving Divination.

Divination

Essentially, using one's psychic abilities to foresee the future for the good of others is called Divination and sometimes "fortune telling"; the tools (beside your psychic abilities and your guides and angels, etc.) for doing Divination are numerous: Tarot-cards, (more on those later) Rune Stones (a set of 25 stones made of clay, marble, etc. with a Viking symbol on each; one is left blank. They are "cast" (or thrown), selected randomly like Tarot-cards and/or placed in a spread or within concentric-circles representing the elements, four directions and other considerations. Astrology and Numerology doesn't require the use of one's psychic abilities but is still a way of predicting future trends. The Pendulum is in a class by itself.

Pendulum

With a pendulum, you can get answers, but whether it swings in various directions because of the influence of guides or spirits on it, or because it is merely a tool for accessing the questioner's own subconscious wherein lies their true answers, is not for me to decide. You must simply try it for yourself and decide. A pendulum can be fashioned from a common builder's plum-line, or any weight (like a fishing-weight) attached to a string or small chain will work. You can use a heavy stone or crystal, or merely buy a ready-made pendulum. Hold the end of the string or chain between your first and second finger, thumb on top of those 2 fingers in such a way that about 2 or 3 inches of the string or chain hangs over the front of your first (index) finger and the chain hanging down from behind your second finger and downward. Make sure the pendulum is completely quiet/stationery. Mentally ask a yes/no question that you know the answer to be "yes" to and watch which direction the pendulum begins to swings in.

(north-south, east-west); you'll know then that any questions you'll ask which are answered "yes" to will swing in that direction! Ask a question that you know the answer to be "no" to and see where the pendulum swings…you'll then have your "no" swing for "no" answers!

Again, only you can decide whether the pendulum responds to a subtle muscular movement based on your own subconscious knowing or if there is something "more" to it.

The Pendulum is also used by some Healers to determine a person's area of concern.

Specifically, holding the pendulum over each of the person's chakras one at a time and seeing if it swings or not is a method used by some. Chakras are inner energy-spots that correspond to major parts of a person's body. For example, there are 7: On top of a person's head or "Crown", their "Third-Eye," "Throat", "Heart", "Solar Plexus", "Naval" and "Root" charka. These spots apparently correspond along the back of the person as well, along their spine, and treating the charkas with Reiki in this way is a very typical Western (or "Non-Traditional") form of Reiki treatment. There are countless more forms of Divination, but for the purposes of discovering and developing your psychic abilities and awareness, the pendulum and Tarot-cards can't be beat. In the following chapter, we will cover in more detail the Tarot: it's uses for divination as well as evolving your gifts.

As well, we will explore further Angels, Spirit-Guides and distinguishing which they are, their relationship to the dearly-departed and doing Mediumship and Channeling in relation to this all.

Let's proceed then, to the next chapter, but remember to continue practicing your "Altered-States" exercises so that you may quicker and quicker enter into that daydream state; if you've not yet met your guides, attempt to do so, and try the playing-card exercise again so that you can see how far you're progressing.

Practical Magic

Putting everything together here creates magic in a sense; you get to explore the Tarot for divination, learn more about entities around you and others (and maybe even see them), and decide the best direction to go for yourself: Healer or Psychic or both?

The Tarot

This is something close to me, because it's how I got my professional start in the area of self-help/alternative health/healing and divination!

Of course, I had a strong grounding in meditation, and matters spiritual and metaphysical. I was already working for many years as a college-trained Graphic Designer among other careers. Although I knew I had the "gift"; applying it to divination and the Tarot did pose a challenge. Especially under "pressure", when I decided to take it out of my home and into restaurants, cafes and dance-clubs. I had to "produce" on "command" for paying customers; I also had the challenge (which later turned out to be an advantage) of very distracting environments! (It was really hard to focus while your favorite dance-music is blaring in the background, and inebriated customers are lined-up to ask such questions as "Will I get lucky tonight?")

Distract Yourself

Once I was out of noisy environments, no longer doing readings, mediumship, etc. virtually out in front of the public's scrutiny (I even "did time"/"paid my dues" 7-days-a-week, 9-hours-a-day doing readings at a public market for 6 years!) it suddenly was much easier. It makes total sense: I was inadvertently training myself/sensitizing myself under harsh conditions/situations, so that when house-parties came along and eventually my private-practice in a quiet environment, doing readings were a "breeze'; hearing my guides was easy; conversing with the dead was a lively affair.

So here's another tip: when practicing hearing/seeing/etc. your guides, or doing any other psychic work, keep your radio or TV loud for the first few months, then try doing all of that in perfect quiet. What a difference that will make. Remember to not think too much, either. Just "go with the flow" and trust what you're experiencing.

I won't give you a history lesson on the Tarot at this point; for that, there are tons of resources at your disposal both in book form and on the internet. Suffice it to say that their origins lie in antiquity; they have been recorded historically at least as far back as medieval Europe (France, for example) as well as Italy during the Renaissance, when they were used by royalty in card-games. Look at what I call "historically-accurate" decks at Metaphysical bookstores; decks like the Tarot de Marseilles (12th century France, colored in the 17th century), the Carey-Yale (Sforza) deck from 16th century Milan, the Rider-Waite deck (1920's England) and see if you are attracted to any of them. They are "clean" and lacking in too much interpretation, unlike the modern "New-Age" decks of today. Even the more recent Aquarian and Connelly decks are pretty acceptable. Just don't use the Thoth deck, a deceptively-beautiful deck created by one of the world's most infamous Satanists Alister Crowley. There are many subliminal messages worked into the art and wording of the names of the cards which are not recommended if you intend to be a "Light-Worker."

Let's get you started right away with your deck; it need not have been given to you as a gift (merely one of many superstitions surrounding the Tarot), but as outlined previously, it is crucial that you get "acquainted" with your cards. Another superstition is that others shouldn't handle them…how ridiculous is that, especially because you want your client's vibrations to affect the cards so that they come out fairly accurate! Besides, you can "clear" the energy in the cards between readings using a symbol from Level 2 Reiki, passing the deck over the smoke of burning Sandalwood incense or sweet-grass. No worries there.

Quick Tarot-Tips

There are easy ways to learn the meanings of the 78 cards of the Tarot. First, know that the 56 cards referred to as the Minor Arcana connect with the modern deck of playing cards: they have 4 suits: Coins/Pentacles or Discs (like the suit of Diamonds, it relates to matters financial and issues of the home and material themes) Cups (like the suit of Hearts, it relates to love and matters emotional) Swords (like Spades it relates to taking action) and finally Wands, Batons, Staves, Staffs, Spears, Sticks (like Clubs, it relates to intuition and inner-strength, sometimes to business) Numerologically, an Ace (or one) relates to new beginnings, a Two means something incomplete or in progress, a Three is completion, wholeness, closure. Fives to Tens are generally optimistic, especially for Cups and Coins, negative and stressful for Staves and Swords. For example, 6 of Cups is optimism in regards to love, 9 of Swords is stress, self-blame and worry. For Pages, it represents a beginner/student of whatever the suit is; Knights (usually depicted on a horse) have "graduated" to jumping on their horse and are moving forward in the area of whatever the suit is; Queens and Kings are both "experts" in whatever the suit is, for example a King of Cups could make a good partner/spouse. Generally Queens are more broad-minded while Kings are narrow-minded/set in their ways. Then there are the remaining 22 cards referred-to as the Major Arcana. The only one that remains from this group in the modern deck of cards is the Joker, evolved from the Fool.

Basically, the Major Arcana represents a spiritual journey starting with 0 or The Fool (or naivete) and ending in 21 orThe World (wholeness, completion, self-actualization) The Magician can "move mountains", The High Priestess represents our pessimistic nature, the Empress is wisdom, fertility, empathy and psychic-ability, The Emperor is wisdom from life-experience, The Heirophant is wisdom from prayer/faith, The Lovers is marriage/commitment, The Chariot is a trip, advancing forward, progress, Justice is Divine as well as legal, The Hermit is strength from independence,

Wheel of Fortune is positive karma, Strength is patience, The Hanged Man is wisdom from suffering, ascension, Death is transition, change, Temperance is pacing oneself, The Devil is an obstacle, The Tower is major change, The Star is good luck, The Moon represents patterns, cycles, The Sun is bright new beginnings, Judgement is self-judgement.

Tarot For Divination

Upside-down cards can be read as the opposite of whatever the card would be right-side up; if the card is already somewhat negative, the upside-down aspect will negate somewhat the negativity!

Without looking at the faces of the cards, try randomly selecting 3 cards, laying them down at first with their backs-up from right-to-left. Turn each one over one-at-a-time starting from the far right. This can be interpreted as past-present-future, the far right card being the past. Another way to do a three-card spread is to deal out the first card representing current-situation; next card represents the route/way to getting to the last card/situation. Whatever makes sense to you; maybe you feel more comfortable dealing the cards from left-to-right instead of in the other direction. It's up to you.

A standard 10-card spread is called the **Celtic Cross Spread** and is very effective. Refer to the booklet that came with your cards to learn this spread.

Start doing readings for yourself, trying to remember the meanings of the cards at first; gradually use your intuition to "feel" the intent/meanings/messages so that you don't limit yourself to the literal meanings of the cards.

Never refer to the booklet/instructions so that you don't grow dependent on it. Eventually when you feel confident, start doing small readings for others: you'll be surprised how accurate your impressions and readings become. The cards just seem to fall into the relevant positions…no-one really knows why. Another superstition states that you shouldn't read for yourself or read more than once a day; I tried reading myself and for others more than once a day, and the almost identical cards kept coming up! Also, it's very difficult maintaining objectivity for oneself, so naturally reading yourself might be discouraged.

Remember this when reading Tarot-cards: get your client/friend/etc. to spontaneously select their cards: I find having them cut the deck once works well…merely pull cards from where they cut. So you see it's just as important for your client to be spontaneous as it is for you to trust your spontaneous impressions. If you're working with your guides by now, have them do the work for you: see if they'll give you information for the client without you having to use the cards; glance around the client's head to see if there are any "angels" (more on them shortly) or spirit-guides present; a dearly-departed may be trying to come through…maybe animals or other gargoyle-like creatures are present? Remember to rebuke silently to see if they remain or not. Go with anything you may be seeing or hearing; you may "see" a date, a name…a scene…anything and everything is valid, and the more you trust that and just say what you're seeing or being shown, the more you'll begin to trust your extra gifts and the easier it will flow! Again, always remember to first clear your space/smudge before doing psychic work of any kind and do your rebuking to confirm that any entities, guides, dearly-departed that appear are "of the light". Try putting yourself into an altered-state first to further "open"/sensitize you.

Angels, Spirit-Guides, Dearly-Departed & Other Entities

Let's assume you're at a point where you can see spirit-entities (don't worry if you can't yet…that takes practice, and it may not be your particular gift…keep putting out the intent and see if it happens one day! _Note_: Seeing auras used to be very popular about 10 years ago; everyone and their dog was either claiming they could see auras and/or asked me if I could. I was never particularly interested in seeing people's auras, so I wasn't paying much attention to them…after all, talking to the dead and other people's guides was enough for me! But one night I decided to "put out the intent"/ "put it out there"/"put it out to the universe" that I'd like to see auras. A couple of nights later, as I lay in bed reading, I noticed out of the corner of my eye a green glow around one of my hands which was holding up the book. I was seeing my own aura! I suspect that putting out that intent/wish/desire previously opened my subconscious to seeing auras as well. I'm still not excited about being able to do this at will (*Other note: you'll have to learn to "turn the "gift" on and off at will, or it will feel uncomfortable to constantly be so "open"; I find consciously pulling in my own aura/visualizing that I am doing that really helps me to not "feel"/see too much when I don't want to.*) I don't have too much use for using auras to determine the state of someone's health (which is so often done) or their personality profile; I can glance over someone subtly and their ill areas stand out as dark-areas on a person to me. If the client gives me permission to see more (and I always ask first!) I'll look right at them, scanning from head to toe in an attempt to see deeper internal illnesses…they appear as deep red and glowing areas inside them. This is one of my gifts…it may or may not be one of yours, and if you can "diagnose" troubled-areas, you mat see them differently than myself; give it a try!

I know I went about my point about seeing guides and other entities and the intent to do so being crucial in a rather long-winded way, but…now you get the point! Just because you may not be able to see/hear something, it could be it's not your particular gift, sure, but also you might just need to put out a subconscious intent to be able to do it!

Back to the Entities

Angels rarely (if any time) look like beautiful winged gods or goddesses. That is merely a Judeo-Christian concept. More often than not, they look "scary": like mutated gargoyle-like creatures, sometimes part-lizard one color, part sphinx another color! Really. I don't do drugs and I'm not schizophrenic. It's true! The more "creative" the client is, the more..."interesting" their angel (I hate that "New-Age" word!) is.

The first clue that there's an angel (please invent another word...) around the client is that the client glows...either their face or their whole head. When I see this, I "unfocus" my eyes as previously described and sure enough, there they are...sometimes one over their head, great gargoyle-like wings spread protectively around the client's shoulders, and sometimes up to 3 or more around each shoulder. Sometimes a dearly-departed is given by God to the client to serve the same protective, extra-luck purpose as an angel. Dearly-departed? They either are there or they're not; either you can see them, or not...don't force it, and don't let a client force you to try and see poor old dead Uncle Moe if he's not there. Another psychic told me once that I can bring the deceased in question (should they not be present) to the client by having the client utter the deceased one's full name three times. I've tried this...it works. But I have an ethics issue there. Why force the dead-person to suddenly come from wherever they are to appear beside your client? I feel there's a "free-will" ethic/issue being ignored there. So I don't do it, nor do I encourage it. If they're not there, they're not there...just admit it. Usually there's a dearly-departed around the person because: the deceased entity believes that the client "needs" them to be there, God "assigns" them there to help the person or for karmic-debt reasons, or they are "earth-bound", or "stuck" around the client, unable to leave and hover around other family-members, usually because both the client and the entity need closure (ie-they need to say a final "good-bye") I recently had a 40-something client who lost her 3 girlfriends in a car-crash when they were all 18; she was supposed to go out with them that night but instead felt compelled to go to one of the girl's homes and say good-bye before doing something else that night. There they were, transparent but obviously 18-ish and around my client! (They appear to me visually in such a way that my description of them helps the client to identify who it is...even if, say, they died at age 63 but look like 34...the client likely remembers them the most easily at the age of 34, for example)

All they wanted to do was say "good-bye" back to my client; they had been earth-bound, unable (in this case) to visit other friends/family-members or "go to the light" (God, Heaven, etc.) or onto their next life. In this case, after their tearful exchanges, I witnessed them turn away and leave, off and upward, I believe to the light, as I saw a golden-glow that they seemed to be headed towards.

Dearly-departed sometimes are assigned as spirit-guides, but more often than not they are more like angels, bringing "good-luck" to the client.

Spirit-Guides we've spoken about previously. They can look odd like angels. They can look like transparent humans, often we "inherit them" from previous lifetimes…so they may appear in period-garb; this is one of their main uses in this case…they can tell us who they were in relation to the client (ie- the client's lover/partner, brother/sister/maid, etc from 18th-century London) and the client can learn more about their own karmic-debts left over from these lifetimes and/or why they are the way they are now based on who they were previously. It's fascinating stuff, very popular, and incredible when I hypnotize my clients privately to have them go themselves to their own past lifetimes. A little different than me psychically "spoon-feeding" them their past-life info with the help of my guides and their's; that's the other thing…always remember to rebuke (to make sure these entities are not deceiving you) and if you can, confirm information by having your own guides elaborate on any info given by these entities.

Sometimes your clients will also have transparent animals of all kinds around them; they are protectors, but their characteristics/strengths are also given to the client.

There you have it.

You may see them, you may not.

Your gifts may be different; you may be able to move objects…divine the future, heal others, pick up "vibes"(impressions) from objects (Psychometry), see auras; it varies from person to person.

Regardless, you are well on your journey along the path of self-discovery and the world of psychic phenomena.

Try to listen over and over to the cd's/tapes so that you can heighten your sensitivity. The deeper you go each time, the more open to psychic phenomena you'll become. Practice unfocusing your eyes, doing the altered-state exercises and meditating regularly if you can.

Just remember: be spontaneous and don't think. Just DO it. That goes for readings, and whatever you're seeing/hearing/feeling…have no doubts…keep saying (almost continuously) what you're experiencing. No psychics nail everything 100% anyway, so why worry? That's how you can tell a fake from the real thing: the more incredibly in detail they give times, dates, places, names, etc., the more likely they have procured the information secretly (believe me, it's AMAZING how a charlatan can do this!) and are bluffing. Television never shows all the "misses" famous psychics have, but believe me, if you've ever attended a live TV-show taping with one of the famous psychics doing readings, they'll edit down to 8-minutes mostly "hits" from the actual 30-minutes of readings done (of many misses along with the hits!) in the studio.

Finally

I'm stating all of this not to put down the pro's, but to encourage you. Please be sure to write/e-mail/phone us with comments, questions, suggestions and most importantly news of your own progress.

Guided Meditation

Here is the previously-mentioned guided-meditation/visualization or induction-script (a term used in Hypnotherapy) here which I used to use in all of my sessions, with some variations to suit the particular purpose of the session. If you want, you can read it aloud, taping your voice as you do so; try to use a slow, steady pace, unemotional and soft speech-pattern; play it back over and over, and it will enable you to go deeper each time so that you may achieve an altered state quicker and easier. Listening to a recording of the script will also provide you with deep relaxation, improve your concentration and memory, and will help your psychic abilities, so that you will eventually be able to achieve an altered state anywhere, anytime without formally having to close your eyes or lay down. I do suggest that when you play back the script on your tape-recorder, that you shut off your telephone and listen to it through head-phones, preferably laying down on your bed or couch with lights out. If you don't have head-phones, that's alright. As long as you set up a private, quiet and peaceful environment, unhindered by kids, spouse and phone-calls.

One more thing: please do not listen to this recorded-script (if you've recorded it) when driving or doing anything that requires your complete concentration; besides the obvious dangers, you won't be doing the script any justice…it's effectiveness will be greatly lessened if you don't give it your complete attention.

The Script

Close your eyes and take a full, deep breath…and exhale. Again…take a full, deep breath, all the way to the bottom of your lungs…and exhale. Do it one more time…a full deep breath but this time hold it in for a second…and now exhale that fresh, clean relaxing air fully, completely and letting go as you do so. Feel yourself relaxing all over.

Now all I want you to do is simply listen to my voice. As you listen to my voice I will ask you to tense and relax certain muscles in your body. If you find yourself distracted from my voice or if you find yourself day-dreaming, don't worry or be concerned. Just return to my voice and continue with this session. I also want you to be aware that should you have any reason why it would be unwise for you to tense a part of your body when I ask you to it is perfectly in order to ignore my request. So now that you are comfortable, let's begin.

The first thing I want you to do is concentrate on your face. Concentrate on your brow. Nod your head if you can feel any tension there. Now concentrate on your eyes and the surrounding area. Nod your head if you can feel any tension there. Now concentrate on your chin. Nod your head if you can feel any tension there. Sometimes because we have tension in certain parts of our body all the time, we accept the tension and do not recognize it as such. It is possible that that there are muscles that are holding tension so we will continue.

I want you to tense as many muscles in your face and eyes as you can-screw up your face and tense as hard as you can. Good-now relax those muscles. Now let's do that again. Tense-relax. Now one more time-tense, and relax. Now.

Now please nod your head if your face feels more relaxed. That's fine, and now I want you to concentrate on your neck and shoulders. Almost everybody has tension in their neck and shoulders and what we are going to do now is to help get rid of that tension. In a moment I will say the word "tense" and then follow it with the word "relax". When I say the word "tense" I want you to push up your shoulders and tense as hard as you can. I will then say the word "relax" and then I want you to drop your shoulders and relax. I'll do this three times. So ready, "tense". And now "relax". Good; now again…"tense"…"relax". One more time…"tense"…and "relax". That's great. You're doing really well, and soon you'll feel the rest of your body also pleasantly relaxed. Now I want you to concentrate on your arms and hands. This time when I say "tense" I want you to tense the muscles in both your arms and hands, either stretching out your fingers or making a fist…whichever you prefer. When I say "relax" just let them flop down and relax. So ready…"tense"…"relax". And again…"tense"…"relax". And one more time: "tense"…and "relax". That's fine…you're doing great. Now I want you to concentrate on your stomach muscles. This time when I say "tense", I want you to tense the muscles in your stomach. When I say "relax", just let the muscles relax. So ready…"tense"…"relax". And again…"tense"…"relax". One more time…"tense"…"relax". That's great. Now we'll go to your legs and feet. When I say "tense", I want you to stretch your legs out and pull your toes up and tense the muscles. When I say "relax", just let them flop down relaxed. So ready…"tense"…"relax". And again…"tense"…"relax". And again once more "tense…"relax". And now I want you to concentrate on your entire body. This time when I say "tense" I want you to tense every muscle in your body. When I say "relax" just let the muscles relax and flop down completely relaxed. So ready…"tense"…"relax". And again…"tense"…"relax". And now for the last time…"tense"…"relax". That's fine and now you're feeling relaxed. Become aware how pleasant the feeling is and also become aware that you can repeat what we have done whenever you wish and return to this pleasant state of relaxation. So continue to enjoy the feelings for the rest of this session. Let's go deeper now, so that you can enjoy the feeling even more. Take a deep breath, hold your breath, and let it all go, relaxing even more. Again…a full deep breath, holding it for a second, then just let it go relaxing even more deeply. Focus on your legs and notice how relaxed and heavy they feel; they're feeling more and more relaxed and heavy. Focus on your arms…notice how loose and heavy they are, becoming more and more loose and heavy, like lumps of lead, completely relaxed, loose and limp, getting heavier and heavier as time elapses. Focus on your breathing, breathing freely and deeply, free and deep. Notice how your breathing is becoming slower and much more deep as you relax more and more. Just let yourself go completely, relaxing more and more with each breath you take. Become aware of how pleasant this relaxed feeling is, and you go deeper with each breath, feeling more and more completely relaxed. Let yourself go completely, the last bits of tension completely leaving your body. Feel your right leg going limp…the muscles in your right leg relaxing more and more completely. And now your left leg, let it relax more and more in the same way, completely limp. And now your right arm, let the fingers, the hand, the forearm go completely limp, relaxing more and more deeply. Now the left arm, let it relax in the same way, more and more completely relaxed. Now your neck and shoulders…let them go limp, completely relaxed. Now your entire body…completely relaxed, loose and limp, relaxing more and more deeply.

Feel the tension leaving every single muscle in your body, from the very top of your head, to the very tips of your toes, completely relaxed, loose and limp.

Notice how great this relaxed feeling is, feeling more and more content, relaxed and comfortable, with a feeling of peace and comfort permeating every inch of your body. As you drift down more and more deeply, relaxed and peaceful, let yourself go with every breath you take. Deeper and deeper, more and more completely relaxed.

I want you to imagine now that you are standing on the top step of a heavy wooden staircase. Feel the carpet under your feet. Now extend your hand out and touch the railing. Feel the smooth polished wood of the railing under your hand. You are standing just 10 steps up from the floor below. The stairs are curving very smoothly down to the floor below. In a moment we will walk down the stairs. With each step down you will allow yourself to relax even more deeply. By the time you reach the floor below you will be deeper than you have ever gone before. Take a step down now, down to the 9th step smoothly and easily. Feel yourself going deeper. Now down to 8, deeper still. Now down to 7...6...5...4...3...2...1. Now you are standing on the floor below.

Before you is a beautiful, shiny, full-length mirror. This is the mirror of truth, and it reflects only the truth. Reach out and touch it now...feel how smooth, light and clean it is. I want you now to see yourself in the mirror. I want you to look at your hair, your face, your clothing, even your shoes in the mirror. Notice the bright golden-white light that seems to shine out from your face, and from your heart. In fact, this golden-white light is shining out from your entire body, top to bottom. This is the golden-white light of a Higher Power, shining through you, and from you, and you can see it. This makes you feel safe, warm and happy; content and secure in yourself and in your future. You're feeling safe, warm, happy, content and secure in yourself and in your future. Nothing can or will stop you now. You feel simply great; beautiful and confident in who you are and what you are doing with your life. You realize now, that you are taken care of, and that others can also see this beautiful, golden-white light radiating out from you, and it makes them feel good about themselves too, and their life. Everytime you want to feel good about yourself and your life, remember this mirror of truth, and how it reflects the beautiful, pure, golden-white light out to the world. How good you look and feel. You will always remember that, and that you are taken care of. You are filled with a new-found faith and confidence in yourself from now on. You can and will remember the mirror anytime you want to, and the wonderful feelings associated with it. In fact, everytime you see a mirror, you will feel good about yourself and your life. Completely in control.

Turn around now, and notice that you are at the foot of your spiral staircase. I will now count from 1 to 10. With each number I say, take one step up your staircase until you reach the top.

1...2...3...4...5...6...7...8...9...10.

You are now at the top of your staircase. The next time you hear my voice in a session either in person, on tape or on CD, you will allow yourself to relax even more and more completely than you are now. And the suggestions I have given you will keep going deeper and deeper and deeper into your mind.

In a few moments when you awaken yourself, you will feel very relaxed, and you will be completely refreshed, alive, alert and full of energy, full of confidence. You will feel simply great. All you have to do to awaken is to count with me silently from 1 up to 5 and at the count of 5, open your eyes, feeling relaxed, refreshed, alert, in very high spirits. Feeling very good indeed.1...2...3...4...5. Open eyes, alert and awake.

There you have it!

I know that the hypnotic-script/guided meditation will be crucial for your practice, and is worth the price of the book alone.

Please excuse any redundancies you may have encountered between the tarot and psychic awareness material, as originally there was a bit of a "cross-over" so-to-speak between the two, in both the workshops and the manuals. Nonetheless, read, re-read, and study the bonus material, as it might be the entire basis for your practice!

8-Designing Business Cards/ Brochures/Web-Pages/ Editing Audio and Video/ Animation, Etc.

For me, this is one of the most exciting chapters of this entire book, because by trade, I'm a college-trained Graphic Designer, with years of experience in marketing and advertising, as well as in illustration, cartooning, and animation.

At this time in history, there are numerous (and infinite) apps and free programs to help you do all of these things! Even this very book was written using a template for a standardized, professional format for print. You can so easily nowadays design a website, with animated "gifs", photos, even animated clips and illustrations, all provided at little, if any, cost to you! You can use a free app on your phone, tablet, laptop, or desktop computer to record audio, or even video, the quality of which is so high, that it is all at a professional level!

Online services, such as what "Vistaprint" (**http://www.vistaprint.com**) offers, can help you design your own, professional quality business cards, brochures, postcards, banners, etc., etc., all for a very reasonable fee.

I was going to go into extensive detail on "how to do" all of the aforementioned and crucial marketing tools, but it looks like I won't have to! I even had someone approach me recently to help her in using these tools, but alas, I fear that my role here is now obsolete! So many design and marketing tools are so readily available and easy to use, that I need not go into any detail in these areas! Alas, even if I do, the apps and programs will probably become obsolete by the time this book is published, and you even read this!

I recently realized that the programs I was going to suggest to my potential students are now considered "old school", and upon my Facebook-messaging her them, she probably had a chuckle!

I still use an old version of *Windows Movie Maker*, mainly because it's free, and it serves me well! For audio-recording, I use the free version of *Audacity*! It provides me with professional results, in many formats. I still use an older version of *Photoimpact*, (before *Corel* took it over) because it uses little space on my computer, and does the exact things that the professional version of *Corel*'s *Photoshop* does! I'm not cheap, it's just that these programs work for me, just happen to be free and serve my purposes, so I use them!

I also use a free "Movie-to-Gif" program, a free, online "Gif-to-Movie" program, a free "Video-Capture" program called "Debut", (which can capture anything on your screen, video or otherwise) the "YouTube Uploader" (or is it "Downloader"?) which can upload to your computer any video on You Tube., plus many other programs which I'm sure that I've forgotten, in order to record and edit all of my social media self-promotion graphics, video, and audio.

So rather than try to teach you how to use even a few programs, and end up writing several more books, I invite you to decide what you need for your purposes, download the apps and/or programs, and go-for-it! If you have a more computer-literate, "techie-friend" to assist you, so much the better!

This is what I did, back-in-the-day!

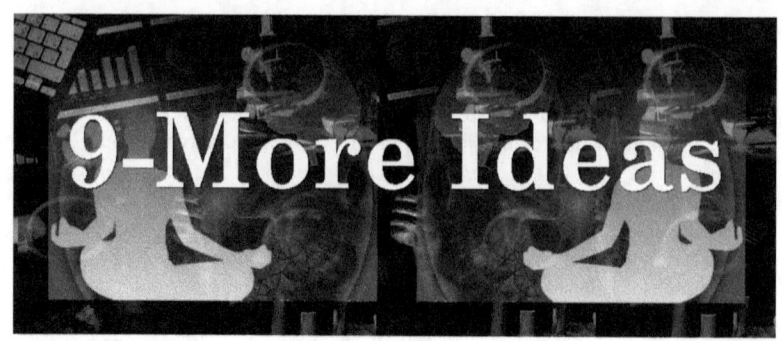

9-More Ideas

Here we'll discuss any additional ideas which I might have previously overlooked.

When marketing yourself and your services, remember to use as many colorful and interesting adjectives as possible. Have a Thesaurus/online Thesaurus handy in case you run out of words. This is particularly important if you're doing your own copy writing and advertising for any ads, newsletters, promotions, etc. you might be distributing. This goes for your website and business cards as well. For example: "This Looks Insane!" "Revealed: Happy Birthday Trick!" "Melting Card Trick Revealed!" "Shocking Card Trick!" These are all titles for magician Jay Sankey's latest explanatory magic-videos, and don't they sound exciting? The titles are attention-getting, even dramatic! This is because of his use of words such as "shocking", "insane", and "revealed". He also uses words such as "mind-blowing", "amazing", and "impossible" to describe his tricks. This is a lot more attention-getting than "card-trick" or "rope-trick", which is all they really are. The descriptions make the videos sound like they're special, and worthy of your attention, because they get your attention right away with the use of certain words.

When I market my videos, podcasts, and webcasts, I use a similar technique. I even do this for my book titles, such as "Break Out Now!", "The Powerful Healing Gift of Prana", "The Four Fold Path to Enlightenment", and "Higher Thought". All of these titles suggest something more than the subject matter actually is, and yet the titles are not misleading. There is always truth in my advertising, and that includes the wording and descriptions, and even in the titles.

This is a knack you either have naturally, or can certainly develop over time and experience; the Thesaurus helps!

More Marketing Ideas

In case I haven't previously mentioned this, so-called "live" "interactive" seminars and workshops are currently all quite popular, and they are generally accomplished through the use of such programs as Skype, Wire, Viper, Google Hangouts, ooVoo, Face Time, Facebook Messenger, and Talky. There are also programs that enable one to have conference-calls, such as Uber Conference and Zoom. In other words, with these programs, you can hold seminars without having to leave the comfort of your home! This saves a lot of money on hall, room, or auditorium space, and is just as professional, nowadays, maybe even more so!

Alternatively, you can offer pre-recorded lectures, workshops, and certification courses, which are just as effective as the online/conference-call or live ones, maybe more so, because your students can keep referring back to the course material, which is on pre-recorded audio and/or video. This would require that you be adept at recording and editing audio and video, but as stated before, with today's Smart Phones, you can turn out amazingly professional-quality audio and video material. All you need do is assemble some promo-material to sell these courses (live or otherwise) on your website and social-media, determine a specific date and time for the live ones, and then use PayPal to receive payment. Make sure (particularly with the pre-recorded seminars) that you add a disclaimer essentially stating that once they've paid for the course, there are no refunds, or else they'll simply download the material and ask for a refund, keeping the material. With live presentations, I ask that no recording devices are used or present, just for the same reason! What's to stop someone from paying, attending the lecture, recording it, and then asking for a refund, hanging on to your material, or worse, posting it for free (or for their monetary gain) on social media? Always state somewhere, "No refunds. No recording devices allowed".

There are numerous incentive-methods for getting people to sign up for your pre-recorded seminars. These include stating that there is a "One-Time Fee", and then "Unlimited Access to All Audio, Video, and PDF (written) Materials". This suggests that they are getting a great "deal". Offering free, one of your books as the course manual is also motivation, and this goes for the live or pre-recorded courses/lectures/workshops. I always do this, supplying either my actual paperback book (relevant to the specific course) or a PDF (downloadable) version of the book.

Some professionals also offer as incentive for signing up/paying for the course(s) a "free", once-a-month consultation. This could vary in length, but never exceeding two hours. This might include a "Q&A", (question and answer) or discussion/debate, or even motivational session. Sometimes it is a coaching session. Whatever you are equipped to do, but which you also feel comfortable to offer/include in your package.

Remember to always have fun, and your patients, clients, and students will too.

Weekend Retreats

This is a fancy term for a series of lectures and workshops that usually take place at a nice resort, usually in the country/rural area. It features a number of different practitioners, for example, Yoga or Tai Chi Instructors, Reiki Practitioners, and others who specialize in previously discussed modalities. There are (for example) 10 lectures/presentations throughout the day, usually starting with a morning meditation, and/or Yoga or Tai Chi.
It is potentially a great opportunity for a large convergence/gathering of New Agers, Spiritualists, Holistic Practitioners, etc.

How would one go about organizing such an impressive endeavor? The structure is identical to the aforementioned Psychic/Wellness Fairs, the location being at a resort, rather than at a hall. Merely phone around (or e-mail) various resorts and ask them how much they would charge for you to lease space there for a weekend; mention that it would include you leasing sleeping quarters for potential clients and students. Pick one of the locations, and then charge accordingly, based on what your lecturers and presenters would charge you for their services. Add on a consideration for food for the weekend: does the resort include food and meals in their price, or must you provide healthy meals and snacks?

Podcasts and Webcasts

Starting your own webcast on You Tube is easy! Pick a topic, use your smart phone, and go for it, uploading the videos onto the You Tube site. If you want a fancy graphic for the title of your webcast, use the aforementioned (free) Photoimpact by Corel, or any art program for this purpose; sometimes this is built into your smart phone and you can quite easily use this function. Hopefully because of your knowledge and experience, you'll have a lot to share/talk about! The same goes for your podcasts.

Usually your smart phone and/or laptop, desktop, etc. will have a built-in microphone, even a recording program! You can use the aforementioned Audacity audio recording program for this, and as for a site to host your podcast, I recommend the free Blogtalk Radio site. It is easy to use! Just record your audio, and upload it, or (even more fun) go "live"! You can do the same with sites such as "Spreaker", "Soundcloud" and "AnchorFM". Again, have fun!

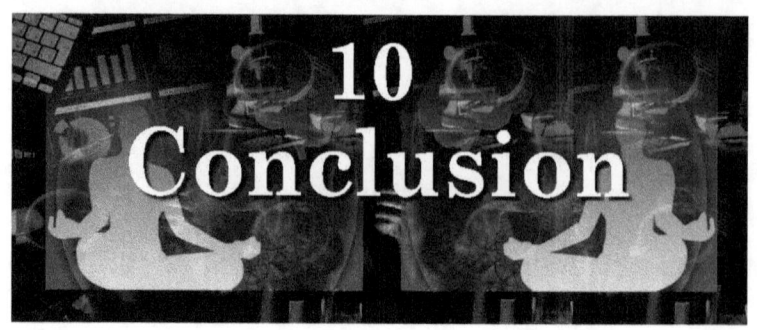

10
Conclusion

I hope you've enjoyed this primer on the business of metaphysics and related genres.

All you need do is remember a few basic things: Be honest with yourself and who you really are. Are you in it for the money, or to actually help others to help themselves? Are you willing to grow along with your clients? Are you open enough to keep learning more and more in regards to marketing yourself? I hope so…it will make your journey a lot more exciting.

Remember the cliché: It's the journey, not the destination. This will help you to avoid frustration, resentment, and disappointment along your journey.

Never stop promoting and marketing yourself first, advertise secondly. With today's social media and accessibility to the world, you are no longer letting others know about yourself and your services locally, but rather globally. You may not pack the auditoriums with your lectures and workshops, but hopefully you're finding satisfaction in the quality, not quantity of the people who attend your meetings, including your Sunday morning gatherings. When you market yourself online, or hold meetings, lectures, workshops, etc. online and through social media, your audience consists of the world, and is unlimited!

Keep studying and earning various degrees and certifications. This is not just because it looks great on your resume and you can charge more for your services and lectures, but because it will broaden your horizons, knowledge-base, and enable you to help more people and more people using more and more tools, or modalities in your tool-belt!

If you absolutely must "earn a living" from this genre:

- Do psychic-readings/Tarot/divination. If you can't, learn how to.
- Organize Psychic and Wellness fairs.
- Sell and market other psychics, practitioners, and lecturers; sometimes it's easier to sell others than yourself!

- Teach what you know and/or do well.
- Become a Clinical Hypnotherapist and help people to lose weight and to stop smoking

Writing books and producing your own (or others') podcasts and webcasts will add to your reputation and elevate you in the public eye, as will your degrees. You can charge others for producing their podcasts and webcasts, once you become adept at it.

I'm sure that once you follow the formulas outlined herein, and begin to earn money and gain notoriety, your career will grow and grow. Before you know it, you'll come up with more ways to market yourself and others, and hopefully, you'll share it with the masses. Always remember to pay it forward.

ABOUT THE AUTHOR

Dr. Michael Likey is an International Author, Clinical Hypnotherapist, Doctor of Theocentric Psychology, Producer/Host of his BlogTalk Radio show, Live-Streamed Video-Broadcasts, and creator of his Transcendence System. He has an H.Dip. (*Diploma of Clinical Hypnotherapy*) from The Robert Shields College of Hypnotherapy, England. Michael is also certified through Robert Shields as a *Fear Elimination Therapist*, (2004) and is also a triple-Doctoral graduate: a D.D., *Doctor of Divinity Specializing in Spiritual Healing*, from the University of Metaphysics, a Ph.D. *Specializing in Mystical Research* from the University of Sedona, and a PsyThD., *Doctor of Theocentric Psychology*, from the University of Sedona, Dr. Masters, CEO. Both the University of Metaphysics, and the University of Sedona, as well as it's parent organization, The International Metaphysical Ministry, were founded by Dr. Masters, CEO. Dr. Michael is the author of more than forty globally-available books on Amazon in addition to dozens of e-books (available on the Amazon Kindle Store), and is also Founder/CEO/Spiritual-Director of his own spiritual gatherings/programs.
He is a Member of the International Metaphysical Ministry and the Association of Ethical and Professional Hypnotherapists.

Contact: dr.likey@gmail.com
Facebook: https://www.facebook.com/Dr.MichaelLikey
Twitter: https://twitter.com/drmichaellikey
YouTube: https://www.youtube.com/user/SoulScienceTV
Website: http://www.drmichaellikey.com

Other Books by Dr. Likey

- **Break Out Now!**-ISBN-10: 9781076531704

- **The Powerful Healing Gift of Prana**-ISBN-10: 9781074017194

- **The Four Fold Path to Enlightenment**-ISBN-10: 1727123239

- **Magic Mike Likey: A Man For All Seasons**-ISBN-10: 172211763X

- **Touched by the Wind**-ISBN-10: 171900062X

- **Higher Thought: Glimpses, Insights, and Snippets**-ISBN-10: 198752070X

- **Reiki: A Legitimate Healing Modality-The Dissertation**-ISBN-10: 1985025515

- **Mystical Meditation**-ISBN-10: 1983952753

- **Affirmative Prayer-Treatments**-ISBN-10: 1983810851

- **Western Psychology Vs. Eastern Psychology**-ISBN-10: 198161091X

- **Spiritual Mind-Science**-ISBN-10: 1973780690

- **How to Pray, Meditate & In-Vision Properly**-ISBN-10: 1973771926

- **Practical Tarot**-ISBN-10: 154840313X

- **Developing Your Psychic Awareness**-ISBN-10: 154839968X

- **Everything is Energy**-ISBN-10: 1548434027

- **Meditation, Metaphysics & Self-Hypnosis**-ISBN-10: 154845138X

- **Hypnosis or Meditation?**-ISBN-10: 1548438987

- **Happiness IS Possible!**-ISBN-10: 1548428736

- **Meditation, Scientific-Prayer & Psychosomatics**-ISBN-10: 1548453129

- **In-Visioning/Imaging**-ISBN-10: 1548007420

- **The Christ Mind**-ISBN-10: 1546539395

- **The Mind of the Universe**-ISBN-10: 1545463816

- **Mystical Wisdom Complete**-ISBN-10: 1543020305

- **Mystical Self-Hypnosis**-ISBN-10: 1542755301

- **Real Problems, Real Solutions**-ISBN-10: 1540447588

- **Mystical Wisdom**-ISBN-10: 1535347775

- **Working Through Trauma Spiritually**-ISBN-10: 1537443100

- **The Mind-The Key to Spiritual Healing**-ISBN-10: 1537319566

- **Dr. Michael's The Key to the Soul**-ISBN-10: 1532946929

- **Dr. Michael's Complete Soul Oracle Cards Manual**-ISBN-10: 1530829623

- **The Complete Spiritual Laws of the Universe**-ISBN-10: 1530735173

- **Speaking Thoughts Into Existence**-ISBN-10: 1517327148

- **Master Reiki**-ISBN-10: 1515026248

- **Dr. Likey's Transcendence System**-ISBN-10: 1514755289

- **Spiritual Mind-Science and Your Soul**-ISBN-10: 1514275104

- **Scientific Prayer**-ISBN-10: 1512183717

- **Journey of the Mind, Journey of the Soul**-ISBN-10: 1440131074

- **The Science of the Soul**-ISBN-10: 1462061885

- **Magic Happens!**-ISBN-10: 059569473X

CD's

- **Affirmative Prayer-Treatments**-
  ASIN: B077Y9YJR2

Testimonials

"I just finished reading your book and I absolutely loved it! I was so inspired and motivated while reading it. Your book is so wonderful and I want you to teach me the tools from your book. I've never emailed anyone after I read their book and I really hope you will reply to this email.
Again thank you for sharing your knowledge and wisdom and I am so thankful I came upon your book in a bookstore."
-Rebecca-

"I have known Rev. Dr. Michael for at least ten years, and I've been grateful to call him both a peer and a friend. In his persistent efforts to help others, he has taken it upon himself to constantly do research (both personal and professional), and to this end he has earned numerous credentials and degrees in his related fields. I have rarely seen him say "no" to assist others, and his professional skills, God-given talents, as well as his consistence to be all he can be has also resulted in him writing several books which I have the privilege of owning.
Dr. Michael shares these ancient and time-proven tools that you'll find are infinitely worth practicing, revisiting, and living for yourself".
-Grace Talson,
www.movingforwardwithgrace.com

"Dr. Likey is an accomplished metaphysician with decades of experience, and in this, his latest book, he shares insights based on his lengthy pastoral and hypnotherapeutic career. This book is a worthy development of that study combining metaphysics with an easy to adopt frame for a better life. I know few people more widely versed in metaphysical study, and it shows in the astonishing variety of influences at play – enjoy!"
-Adam S. Adams, CPC MH CISH CHt.

"Dr. Likey challenges and encourages new methods of self-exploration and discovery through new and ancient wisdom. His unique take on classic and modern therapy and techniques leaves the reader with a greater understanding of mind and soul. His information is both practical and simple to implement into your life. Dr. Likey's personal writing style makes for an easy and interesting read".

-**Sara Adams**, Owner, Finding Avalon - Spiritual ReConnection through Avalonian Archetypes
www.finding-avalon.com

"You've...helped me transcend much of the fear I was living with when I first started coming to the gatherings on Sunday mornings-I feel quite fearless now...you've helped reinforce the value of life/living for me through your tireless work. Thank you again."
-S.K.

"Rev. Dr. Michael is the amazing host of Dr. Michael's Soul Dialogue radio show. I had the privilege of being a guest on his show and was touched by his insight into the history of spirituality, relationships' dynamics as well as his deep knowledge of the human soul. I truly believe that Dr. Michael is providing a great show that can help people in their personal growth and spiritual search."
-Milena Cerin

Top Qualities: Personable, Expert, High Integrity
"Dr. Likey brings a mixture of new thought, traditional psychology and parapsychology to his client sessions. He approaches his work with consideration to all aspects of the clients situation and goes the extra mile to ensure his councel is complete and comprehensive. I recommend Dr. Likey's services in combination with alternative healing (e.g. acupuncture, naturopathic, light therapy), and traditional mental/emotional therapy, as well as for lighter "am I on the right track" counsel."
-L. Miller

Top Qualities: Great Results, Personable, Good Value
"I have attended a number of Michael's meditation evenings where I had a great number of experiences being guided through my spiritual development. I found Michael to be very intuitive, patient and perceptive of his clients needs. I have also worked with Michael doing healing work and I learned quite a bit from his extensive knowledge and practical skills."
-M. Chong

Top Qualities: Great Results, Expert, High Integrity
"Dr. Likey's abilities in the metaphysical field are unmatched in my opinion, his ability to provide insight into your life will amaze you. Dr. Likey provides many other services to enhance your life, seminars, Reiki therapy, and many books related to living a better life.
I highly recommended visiting Dr. Likey."
-T. Hobbs

Top Qualities: Great Results, Personable, Expert
"I was privileged to study Reiki under Mike's expert care, and was astounded by the depth of knowledge that he has on all matters metaphysical.
 The ability to turn the arcane into the comprehensible and digestible is rare, yet Mike has it in spades.
 His personal qualities are outstanding, and the whole experience of learning from him was enjoyable and deeply rewarding. Michael is a great teacher - knows his stuff, he takes research and experience and blends them seamlessly into practical and fun trainings."
-S. Adams MH, CHt

"You are truly a Master and have shown this over and over... God bless and reward you".
-Patti

www.ingramcontent.com/pod-product-compliance
Lightning Source LLC
Chambersburg PA
CBHW072221170526
45158CB00002BA/693